THE FACE OF WAR

Every picture and every word in this book is the work of Charles and Eugene Jones as war correspondents for the National Broadcasting Company Television News. The photographs are enlargement prints, each from a motion picture frame of 16mm film with a negative area of less than one-half inch, as it was exposed on Bell & Howell Filmo newsreel cameras. They are unretouched. Selected from 26,000 feet of combat footage taken during the first five months of the war in Korea, this is the first time 16mm movie film, used as still photos, has been presented to illustrate combat. *To show the face of war . . . to catch the peak of action . . . to stop men in motion . . . to model the high point of their lives . . . and their deaths.*

THE FACE OF WAR

CHARLES AND EUGENE JONES

PRENTICE-HALL, INC., NEW YORK

1951

PREFACE ON WAR 6

CHAPTER ONE RETREAT 8

TWO LINE OF DEPARTURE 26

THREE MASSACRE ON HILL 303 44

FOUR RAIN 56

FIVE SEAWALL AT BLUE BEACH 66

SIX THE ROAD TO SEOUL 82

SEVEN STREETFIGHTER 114

EIGHT AIRBORNE ASSAULT 122

NINE BAYONETS BEFORE SARIWON 136

POSTSCRIPT BIVOUAC 164

ON WAR

A MAN once said that war was ninety per cent waiting and ten per cent fighting. Perhaps. But here are some newsreel clips and a few captions which might tell of that ten per cent and its lowest common denominator, the foot soldier.

A story of combat. A story with no beginning and no ending. For in combat there is only the moment. To the man who must carry the rifle forward, who must live in his hole in the ground, who must think, fight, be killed, all else is nonexistent . . . prologue.

Correspondents are only transients on a battlefield, the journalistic hobos of war, drifting from one point of impact to another, searching, seeking, trying to explain, trying to tell a world only vaguely understanding. Sometimes a camera helps.

Here we can't give the big picture, the weighty evaluated opinion of strategic movements, or tell a massive over-all story. Only of a series of minor incidents and obscure actions played out at seemingly unimportant little positions along a bitter road that was mapped in blood by the infantrymen in Korea. Combat. A people and a place. A way of life.

The place. Most any old place will do. A hillside slope, or a valley pass, or merely the fringe before an open field. That's hardly important. It's no trouble to find. Easy. Get in a jeep, start forward, pass the CP's, corps, division, regiment, battalion. People start yelling, "Get the hell away . . . bastards . . . draw fire." Dismount. Move out afoot. Start to see the long pigstickers on rifles and no tape on rings of grenades at their belts. Reach company. People half buried in the ground. All looking one way, talking into radios, listening, observing, planning. Sprint, slide on your belly. Over the next hill or, zigzag, across the next field. See the animals at work in their holes, hear the noise, smell the smells. That's it, brother. The end of the world.

And wherever it is, it's rain, mud, heat . . . freezing. It's blood on the bayonet . . . murder in the heart . . . and it's wet, warm urine trickling down a leg while little muscles twitch and jump and knot, saying "wait . . . don't . . . watch out." It's a dark and bloody ground you can't know unless you're there. A jumping-off place . . . a rendez-vous for assault companies . . . a point of final departure. The people who live in this place know it only as . . . the line.

The people. They are just ordinary people like you and us, doing what to them are ordinary things in an ordinary place. Sometimes they are a lot, sometimes a very few. Mostly young fellows . . . youngsters who often wear the faces of tired, aged recluses. They lie in the earth, crawl around, fire off rifles, throw things, yell, scream, whisper . . . occasionally wonder why it was they who were chosen. It's not a big involved deal. Just an ordinary thing. No sense getting excited, emotional . . . interested about them. Their faces change rapidly. Morale. Hell . . . no rear echelon general or USO show. But the big things in life, "what kinda grenades we gettin', frag or personnel?" and "who's on our flank, them people from Baker?" Time. Last year was five hours ago when that big mortar knocked out the company CP, and tomorrow will be the same, and the day after.

Sometimes, though, it seems that for all your life you've crouched behind a tank, peered over a ridgeline, lain in a ditch, watched these people going out. Faces, weapons, sound of their feet. They stare at you and you stare at them, and perhaps you turn away and feel like a damned fool because you're crying a little and you don't know why. Maybe it's just for the look of them.

In Korea as in other places, we have looked long into their faces. We saw fear, bewilderment, anger . . . dignity. There are no others like them. They are alone. Men of the rifle companies.

Sometimes we were with these people in that place. It was always a proud thing.

CHARLES and EUGENE JONES

Frankfurt in Germany

7

RETREAT

RETREATING is always a hell of a mess. The confusion is expensive. Costly in time . . . material . . . blood.

This was a new war. Untried, scared troops facing hard battle-trained veterans, outnumbered twelve to one. Attempting a fighting retreat through the hills to the south. Most of them had been lolling at guard duty in Japan a few short weeks before. Suddenly, shockingly they were thrown into the breech of violence. America was a thin line of tired riflemen running back over the hills of southern Korea.

Yongdong was a bad place. A dot on the map, a few dwellings on the road of retreat from Taejon. Crackerbox tanks, lightweight and pitiful against enemy armor, rattled through the deserted streets to take up defensive positions. A regiment elected to make its stand in the rice fields, the paddies before the town. It was not to be. The men were still green, still seeking the low rather than the high ground, still herding like frightened sheep and dropping at the sound of our own shells passing over them. The Reds probed forward, drew our people out, then . . . hit them on the flanks.

A retreat was unavoidable. There were too few left. Taejon had been costly. Squads where there should have been companies . . . companies in place of whole battalions . . . trying to stretch a tight

band of defense across the land. We saw troops, bloody holes in some, eyes bulging, panting, dazed and uncertain, pulling back without orders; occasionally as units, but more often just scared men running down a road yelling.

"The gooks are coming . . . get the hell out!"

Like prairie fire the panic spread until whole sections of the front were in movement . . . backwards. Drab brown figures that were the enemy crawled over the horizon behind them.

A hundred yards up the main street of Yongdong was infantry. Not deployed, just sitting, or lying in ditches on either side. A man, dirty, unshaven, eyes caked with sediment and powder, sat near us, his ragged dungarees, like those of the other men, wet to the waist from running through the scum of the rice paddies. We asked how far the line was . . . what people of ours were there. He answered irritably.

"This is the line, buster . . . there ain't nothing out there but gooks . . . we're the last of the last."

Nearby somebody bawled loudly . . . commandingly. He rose, reached down, picked up his rifle . . . merged into a moving column.

We lay in the ditch watching as they filed silently past. There was no talking, only the rattle of accoutrements marking their passing. Sullen, perplexed faces stared vacantly down at us. They shuffled by, only

11

their eyes and the tips of bayonets bright. We looked away. It is always painful to see one's countrymen in defeat.

Moving among them, we passed through the streets of the place known as Yongdong. Snatches of conversation could now be heard, the voices sounding like old coins, seldom used, seldom seen, rattling about in a rusty piggy-bank. Voices mumbled, coughed, muttered.

"Yeah and that ain't all they going to give us . . . knew he was still alive out there . . . left 'em with grenades 'side the stretchers . . . place, call it Yongdong."

We stopped in front of a single battered brick building. Its roof had been partially ripped away. Inside, battalion aid was packing up fast. Shells passed overhead, and men threw themselves to the dust of the roadway in flat dives. They rose slowly . . . some grinning out of the corner of their eyes . . . holding sheepish debates as to how "that was outgoin', tell you . . . No 'tweren't . . . was incoming I tell ya'." Minutes later battalion disappeared. Jeeps hurrying, lurching from side to side. The sound of their motors died away and there was only the eerie quiet of a burning and deserted town. Its people had long gone. The stench of death was heavy in the air. A rabbit hopped across hot ashes in search of safety, and a half-wild dog, crazed by concussion, bounded after it—the law of survival. A tiny squeak was heard as life left the furry body. A church steeple, cross still atop it, stood out plainly against oily smoke drifting across the skyline.

Two men crouched by the side of the road with us. A bazooka lay beside them. One took rockets out of their long slender cardboard containers and began methodically to lay them in an even line behind the weapon close to his hand. We were at a road junction. Shattered windows, the empty eyes of barren buildings stared at us. It was hot and there was no breeze. Shirts glued to backs. Enemy artillery flashed overhead, burst among the buildings to our rear. The man with the bazooka finished his task as if preparing for the opening of a roadside stand. Turned to his partner in enterprise, wondered about customers, mumbled, "Wished to hell Dog company would show . . ."

They scanned the side street to their left and sighed gustily as little figures approached. They moved at a trot. The Army of the United States, pulling out; now hurrying past, muttering.

"Let's move, boy . . . they're on our flanks now . . ."

The business partners closed up shop, picked up their wares and the four of us joined the last two platoons of Dog company as they stumbled from the town. Farther to our rear we passed a small stable, a few feet off the road. Ammo lay stacked in evenly spaced piles amid the manure. A vehicle had been backed up near the stable to bring out the shells at the last minute. A three-quarter ton, it had taken a direct hit. The rear half was blown off and in the scattered metal and scorched rubber were pieces of what once had been two men. The front sagged on the rims of its now tireless wheels, burning fiercely. The blackened torso of a figure sat upright, bony hands upon the steering wheel as if even in death he would drive his flaming carryall away. We yelled to a passing jeep. It slowed down. We scrambled aboard. Never taking his eyes from the road, the driver slammed his foot against the accelerator, picked up speed . . . asked . . . "How far you going?" And we replied, "All the way."

Days passed. A succession of journeys to the South. Burned and bullet-torn trucks littered the way. Blasted field guns. Debris smoldered, carpeted roads and valleys. An occasional body, arms stiffly outflung, legs curled as if stopped suddenly in the act of a sprinter lay among the roads. Units were strung out over miles of hills and nameless trails whose locations were seldom plotted on the outdated maps.

More figures running through rice paddies . . . more dead and deserted villages. A moment of eternity as we lay on a wooded slope . . . watched mortar fire blast right on top of a five jeep recon patrol sent back into a town. Smoke lifted—one single jeep, careening wildly, tore up the road. Its driver, Corporal Lester Marks, Army Signal Corps, hunched over his wheel. Shrapnel bursts lifted dust from the roadway all along his path as he sped toward us. It was unbelievable that he would make it through. Seven men, nearly all wounded, had managed to cling for three-quarters of a mile on that jeep. They hung sacklike, vomiting blood, eyes tightly closed as he roared on.

We looked down the road from where he'd come. One more man of the recon was to make it out. We saw a tiny wavering figure, trudging out through the dust. One arm hung loosely. Slugs from the village reached for him hungrily. Midway he stooped, slumped slowly into the ditch. Two riflemen went out . . . weaving up the defile. They took him under the arms . . . hustling him back to our slope. His shattered arm spurted blood as they dressed it in the safety of a fallen wall below us.

Black nights, sudden gunfire . . . flares drifting down. Distant sound of bugles, blinking green and red lights, probing. Frantic whis-

perings, figures lurching up out of nowhere, crashing by through underbrush, croaking grenade fragments of words, ". . . coming . . . coming
. . . take off." Panting away into nothingness.

One place . . . quiet . . . deserted, unforgettable in its loneliness. An artillery emplacement, to the north of Taegu, we passed it one
morning going up. The line was only a mile or so forward. Gunners
swarmed about their pieces which poked skyward from a small bowl
between knobs of a saddleback ridge. It was just an ordinary emplacement, nothing special. Later in the day, just a few hours later, we heard
shellfire, looked to our rear, saw dirty brown smoke mushroom up from
the little valley. It didn't drift out, it rolled, billowed, surged up over
the terrain behind us. We knew then the gooks had the place zeroed in,

were pounding it into submission, knocking out our artillery support. Going back, we came to that place. It was a mass of direct hits. The hand of a giant had come down from the sky, pounded, pounded, pounded the area, taken his fingers, dug savagely, gouged and ruptured the earth, ripped it beyond all comprehension. Korea is a stinking place. The warriors slept beneath their gunbarrels which slanted askew and upturned. Their bodies had opened up. As under fission they had opened up, splattered, in their protest had thrown long ropey white strings of things out from the flesh. They steamed in the sunlight. There were many of them. There was no sound except for wind sighing in through the pass and the distant popping of fire fights on the line.

All around in holes and the scooped and blasted cavities which had been gunpits, lay shattered rifles, bits and pieces of equipment, clothes. Skivies, dungarees, even socks, freshly washed that morning from the creek, hung flapping and riddled on sticks, moving alone in the breeze against the drabness of sudden death. Across the road a rifle company, taking up position, pulled in. The old men down

from their hills. They slumped, collapsed in a long double row down the ditch. Few looked across at what had been division artillery.

We wanted water. Closed with them. Near the end of the bank several sat upright. We noticed them, heard the sound of their talk. They were unbelievably filthy and haggard. Big one, little one, always in infantry together are the pairs. Smaller one, back against the bank, slouched ragged and sullen, picking at treasures hanging from his nose as dust from passing vehicles on the road above settled in a film inside throats, up into nostrils, sandlike and grating. Sweat ran in oily rivulets as from a faucet from under his helmet, dripped down chin. He was just another rifle carrier, except for his shoes. They distinguished him. He had laces but they hung slack, untwined from loopholes on either foot while the combat boots gaped wide and lasciviously like the mouth of an old man. We wondered how he could run in them. The other, the larger, was one of those. Tall, bony, dark jowls, hollow cheeks, sitting upright, pack still clamped viselike on back, bandoleers crisscrossed, sagging and almost empty across his chest. A few clips stuck in strap

19

webbing, two grenades planted precise and centered where canteen belt covered belly button. Morphine syrette peeping from under helmet liner. He was all gray-black slime and high animal smell. One of the angry ones. Uncaring, dedicated . . . fierce in their business methods. The killers. Thank God for them. His was the face of war. He drifted a butt up to mouth, didn't puff at it, drooped eyelids, looked long at nothing in a far-off place, considered it thoughtfully. His rifle, muddy, battered, breech clean and very shiny, lay cradled up against one shoulder. The other hand rubbed, squeezed, stroked the metal as the flesh of a lover feels for another. A sniper-scope rode low on its barrel. We asked for water. Sniper-scope looked at Shoelaces, said, "Slide over there and

get us all some water, Jesse," this with a nod towards the dead place behind us.

Shoelaces looked up, rubbered lips, grunted only, "Fug you—fug us all—that's what they're doing," moved his feet in their prisons, busied himself at nose, turned away.

Sniper-scope said nothing, waited, kept rubbing his gunbarrel. After a long while rose, kept his hand close to the end sight of his weapon, dragged it up over the bank behind him. We watched as he moved about there, pausing, stooping over the bloated indignant figures among the debris across the road. He came back, sat atop the bank, slid down in his own little avalanche of sand and sweat stink. Drank deep, put a bent tarnished canteen on the ground. Half a sock covered its bottom. Shoelaces removed a searching finger from nostril, inspected it for bullion, deposited a particle beneath abdominal appendage, scratched quickly. He reached unlooking for the canteen, put it to mouth, sucked noisily. Replaced it between them. Sniper-scope looked across, murmured, "Jesse . . . Jesse, I'd shit green for some K's now . . . wyan't you just slide over there and forage us some now?" this last with a harsh note.

Shoelaces looked angrily around, twisted prying finger savagely in its search, slitted filthy cave of mouth, spoke around upraised palm, "My feet never hurted like this in St. Pete or no place," then twisted up, pulled himself tattered and reproving over the bank, impetuous finger still at its assigned task, as he moved among the rutted dead beyond. Across his back, purple ink loud against stained dungaree read clearly, "Florida—Land of Sunshine." Sniper-scope watched him, stroked his barrel, his talk dribbling out, "Cool . . . cool as ice . . . oughta seen him in Taejon with them shoes . . . man." He reminisced. We got our drink, moved away. Left them there, waiting and patient from their long running.

Word filtered down through the ranks. The commanding general from the seclusion of a fast-moving headquarters had issued a statement to his men: .

"I have only one order for my troops . . . Forward!" it said, then finished briskly, "Stand, or die if you must . . . you will not retreat another foot."

The next day we were with the remaining units of two broken regiments lying on the hills above Kumchon. We watched them pile into trucks . . . abandon their heavy gear . . . move back. They made twenty-two miles that day.

Their goal was the Naktong River. Hours later we saw the thin steel threads of the railroad and highway bridges which spanned it. As we passed over, engineers already scampering monkeylike among its girders were planting the demolition charges. We stopped and watched as truck after truck passed over. Huge vehicles pulling artillery, crammed and heavily loaded. Jeeps and a few remaining tanks swerved by. A tide of faces flowed in. They were a mass of duplication. Covered with crusted masks of sweat-stuck dust, staring blankly and unseeing through goggled eyes they seemed like rigid puppets on a threadbare stage. It grew late and we moved to a small hill behind the bridge. The last company came across followed by a torrent of refugees making a last-minute dash for safety. A low continuous moaning sound reached up to us . . .

Our people had to fire down the bridge, over their heads, to keep

them back, stop them from coming over. Whole units of an enemy could have been with them. Peasant cloth makes a quick uniform. They disappeared down the river bank.

The span was now empty except for two figures in its center. They bent down, made pulling motions at the base of a girder. Rose suddenly and sprinted to a jeep, moved quickly away. Our eyes remained on the deserted bridge. With a roar it disappeared in a blinding flash and as the billowing cloud of smoke settled we saw that its center was ripped apart.

23

Men dug in around us. Machine guns were set up and ammo fed into them. The sound of bolts throwing steel into firing chambers sounded cold and crisp in the dusk.

Hard-faced men raised field glasses.

Far across the river on the distant hills the first brown specks began to appear.

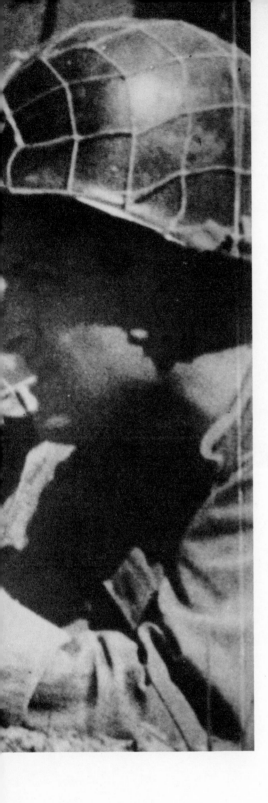

line of departure

SHELLFIRE blasted the valley. White phosphorus clouded the distance with puffballs of death. To the front, one of our new heavy tanks slowly, methodically, threw out round after round of fire. Behind it, twisted half off the road, lay an enemy tank knocked out a few hours earlier.

This was the "bowling alley" of the Naktong River line where for the past month the battered 27th Infantry Regiment had taken everything the gooks could throw at them, and had held. The little valley was littered with knocked out and burned enemy tanks. Villages, charred and smoking, looked vague and indistinct in the haze. Week-old rotting corpses of enemy dead who had come in with their tanks dotted the gashed fields.

We lay on a little rise beside the road, resting among the weary survivors of those who had stood off the previous night's attack. The gooks had sent four heavy tanks rumbling down the bowling alley in the predawn darkness accompanied by infantry. Dirty ragged riflemen, eyes red-rimmed, talking in jerky nervous sentences, told us of the scene of a few hours ago . . . of how in the warm darkness they had heard suddenly . . . roaring motors . . . yells . . . seen gun flashes searching a few feet from their holes . . . fought back with rifles, bazookas and grenades . . . our tanks dug in along the roadway behind them

27

firing point-blank at the winking lights in the gloom. Wild nightmarish moments as explosions rocked the valley. In the light of burning tanks they could see tiny figures tumbling off, running in every direction. Dawn came slowly. They had held again.

One bearded rifleman sat listlessly upon an emptied grenade box. On a stick he twirled a shiny ration can, round and round it went, the sun flashing silver on its side. His eyes followed it without seeing what he was doing. He said mildly, grinning at the can, "It was a cinch . . . just like shooting ducks."

A few feet away a figure slouched in the bottom of a hole. Head buried against his chest he seemed to be dozing in the sun, but then slowly he rose. A 3.5 Bazooka and many opened rocket containers lay about him.

"Yeah . . . just like shooting ducks," he said, looking off down the bowling alley. ". . . except the fuggin' ducks was shooting back."

A few days later we went east to the coast. Rumor had it a big push was starting from Pohangdong. There, earlier in the summer, our people had been pushed from their line in the hills . . . pinned up and held on the flat plain of the airstrip.

After an all day ride over the mountains, we passed through the ruins of that place at dusk shortly after a tank column had cut through to the airfield. They had met little resistance.

The attack was to start the next day. It was a five-phase assault operation involving a regiment of the 24th Infantry Division which had fought gallantly, made a fighting retreat from the north, blooded its units in bitter actions up and down the length of Korea since the first week of war. Their Colonel, tough, sun-burned, his bald head shining in the twilight, speculated about his plans. His infantry would join tanks at a junction point, fight up the main road . . . seize a strategic hill guarding a valley pass. He expected trouble . . . thought resistance would probably be stiff. His voice was hard, flat.

"They will hurt my people," he said.

Next morning just after sunrise we started up the road through the hills. Halfway, the tanks started coming up from their bivouac on the airstrip. As the second one passed, grinning tankers waved, beckoning us. We ran . . . jumped to the turrets. The big shifting vehicles lumbered up the road, bouncing wildly. We felt the weight and power as the big 90mm rifle swayed out in front of us. Walking infantry

laughed and thumbed their noses. We felt good. The air was crisp and not a cloud was in the blue sky above us. It seemed like the start of a wonderful day.

Troops began coming off the slopes as we reached the jump-off point for assault companies. Momentarily the tanks stopped. The riflemen lay in the ditches as our artillery preparation thundered into the hillside ahead. A few got up . . . stood crouched . . . anxious and curious . . . peeping around the lead tank. As the fire support sent from Pohang lifted we moved out, each tank with men walking in file behind or alongside, bending low. Soon we heard the 50cal on the turret of the lead tank let go, then the heavy slam of its big gun. Overhead the air suddenly became alive with unseen whispering. It was a familiar sound. Apparently plenty of gooks were still somewhere on that slope. A man ran past, pants legs flopping in motion.

"Ah right . . . get it up, get it up . . ." he kept yelling, then we heard more shouts. "First section move out."

"Let's get the hell going," some people were saying plaintively to our front.

Those behind the tanks hunched over in the road, as if bearing

great weights and pressed down by time. Their faces became indrawn . . . blank . . . almost elderly. Eyes were pin-pupiled . . . distant. They made mechanical preoccupied gestures about their persons, fastening, unfastening things, inserting clips . . . jolting bayonets on rifles . . . looking out at their world. A world symbolized in clean blue lines on a map in some rear echelon CP, marked only as "line of departure." We heard firing on our left flank. The South Korean division supporting us was up. Riflemen moved out from the road . . . we saw them . . . spread out in a thin line they trotted forward. Their yelling and the sound of their rifles drifted back, heard dimly over the hammering of the heavy machine guns of the tanks. To the right of their line, a big figure, probably their first sergeant, was taking them in, waving them up the slope. We ran to get up to them. That hill was steep. Flopping into a shell hole fifteen feet from the ridge line, we saw in front of us fast-moving and indistinct figures seemingly running in every direction. Some lay flat and fired down the valley. Others knelt, taking aim slowly at unseen targets and spaced their shots. A voice to our front said, "Where the hell are them gooks?"

Without warning a string of mortar shells dropped among us, right

33

down the ridge where everyone was firing. With perfect accuracy "them gooks" had placed their fire on top the ridge line, right in on the first assault wave positions. They apparently were TOT (time on target), for the whole string landed at once.

We were yelling to three youngsters in a hole fifteen or eighteen feet in front of us, to the right, at one boy who had turned his head to us when we saw the small silver sheen of the shrapnel net opening around him; the shell had hit the side of his hole. Then instantly we were in a dust cloud billowing up and around for twenty feet about. But through the dust we glimpsed his body, saw it pinwheel up four or five feet and land off to the right. The two men in with him, killed instantly, were mashed down in the hole. Another youngster, who had been firing on the other side, had his arms riddled, his jaw almost completely blown off.

The whole thing took about fifteen seconds. The dust settled, our heads lifted from the grit of the hillside, and we saw something flopping like a wild thing a few feet from us, the boy with the jaw gone, in a mad dance of pain.

All up and down the line came hoarse cries for medics and help. Some riflemen started running down the hill, but most of them stayed in place.

The hillside was pinned down. We looked at each other, "First time like Iwo . . . a break we only got that one string."

We tried calling for litters. Again men were firing. A few were on their feet, trying to peer over the ridgetop. Again fire flashed above us. A single round had come in, landing short of our line of holes. Simultaneously as it slammed into the ground with a sound of heavy ripping cloth, shell fragments whined. Two figures were silhouetted in front of us. One seemed to stumble . . . his body blurred. His helmet was gone. He sagged at the knees and bent to the ground as if kneeling before some unseen deity. His clutching hands managed to grasp the

arm of the other man as he went down. Time seemed to stand still. We heard in the silence an excited, demanding, fear-stricken voice, "Oh goddam . . . Christ . . . medics . . . medics . . . up here," it pleaded, then fiercely as we saw him pointing, "goddam you . . . come . . . up here . . . and . . . help . . . me . . . with . . . him."

A South Korean soldier darted from the bushes beside him, to help. Expecting more mortar fire they grabbed the injured man, rushed him, half carrying, half dragging, down the hill. Once more they went up at a run, brought down the boy with his jaw gone. A few seconds later over the ridge, crawling and sliding, came a figure with half his dungaree jacket blown off. He reeled among us, his big body thudding into the ground as he fell.

Again we tried calling for litters. We were halfway back down the hill in a little defile, and dust puffs from snipers were once more kicking up dirt just above us. We could make out our mortar men working on the road below. Finally our voices reached them. One paused, turned, walked crouching and scowling to the foot of the hill, cupped his hands to mouth.

"Now just what's important . . . getting them wounded guys out," he bellowed, "or trying to knock out them mortars that got you people."

Above us a boy lay . . . relaxed . . . quiet . . . dead. A rifleman crept past, sliding down the hill looking for medics or litters. We saw him steal a jeep from the mortar men, head back down the road t battalion aid.

We lay in the sun. The three wounded boys wanted water, but because of their throat or abdominal wounds we couldn't give them any. We were isolated on a lonely island of pain with three bloody G.I.'s. One grimaced, finally cursed, lighted up a cig, the other, a slim youngster, the one we saw hit, his throat a torn bloodied mess covered by an aid packet, lay back on the coral-white grit of the hillside as if sleeping, only his eyes remained open. The boy with his jaw torn off arms gashed, riddled, was momentarily restless, sat up, then flopped back in the grass, making vague pain-filled gestures with his hands as if commanding us all to act quickly, to do something, anything.

One of those who had helped bring in the wounded slid over to him. Apparently they were all from the same platoon. He held the dying boy in his arms like a mother comforting her young. His voice rose and fell in a litany of love.

"Oh Sully, they got you . . . Sully, what a damn shame," he murmured.

Then the boy slipped a few inches down into the grass, turned his head to one side. We looked away as he died there, wondering why the overworked medics and their life-saving plasma couldn't have been a few hundred yards closer to our little hill.

No one said anything for a while. The firing above somehow seemed far off and remote. A sand fly buzzed nearby. The boy with the bloody throat, who seemed to sleep with his eyes staring and wide open, rolled over, adjusted his helmet, rolled back and was quiet.

After an interval, a runner came up toward us, yelling that medics were on the way. They followed a few feet behind. They announced the passing of the boy with no jaw.

A medic gave a shot and some water to the two other wounded One rose immediately, almost proudly, waved away a proffered stretcher and disdainfully started down the trail. He had no throat but his gestures were eloquent. He had rested, and the road back had been shown to him. He was ready to go now. A big man, blood streaking down his shoulder blades. We saw him walk off through the waist-deep grass fronds below us. The youth with the other throat wound was at first placed on a stretcher, but after a drink of water decided he, too would go out as walking wounded.

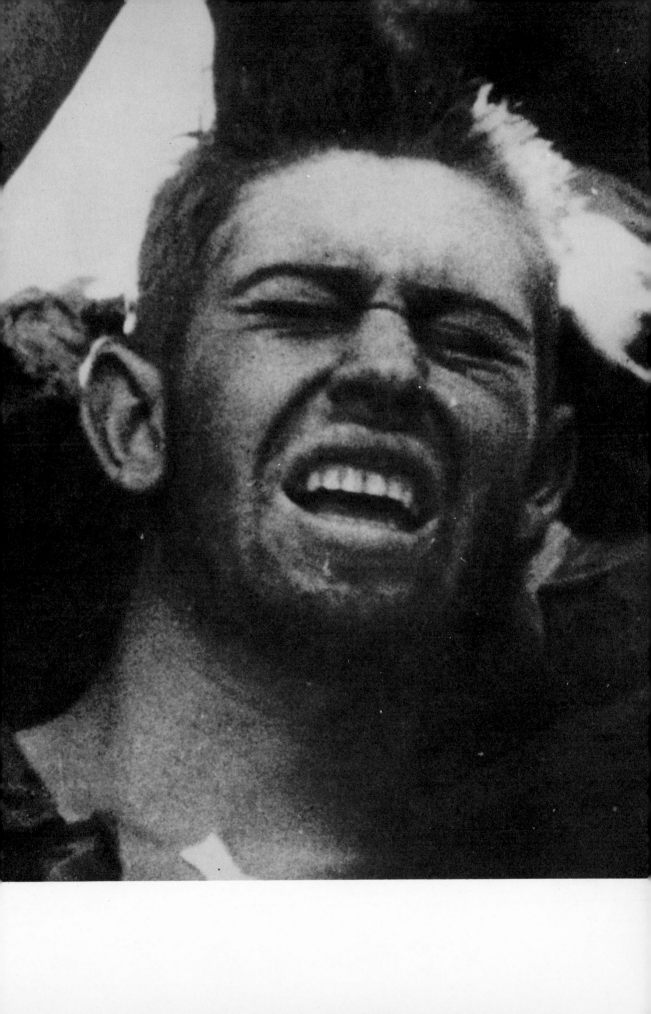

They started off down the slope.

One of the aidmen stayed. He stooped, squatted as if about to relieve himself on the grit, drew knees up under chin. Meditated, dungarees caked, slimy with sweat and other things, mud atop layer of skin, beard, scraggly, black and greasy.

"Charlie company ain't happy up on that mound today," he said out of unmoving lips as the face gravely contemplated bloody splotches on skin. He leaned, dripped spit, hesitant and sticky on the back of a hand. Rubbed slowly. The splotches didn't come off. Hollow, far away, a voice came up from the dung stench of the paddies below.

"Where's the kid?" it demanded, then insisted, "Kid . . . hey, kid . . . get your ass off that hill, Boone's been hit here." Then angrily again, "Kid! . . . hey kid, get your ass . . ." We looked at him, knowing, remembering others, the "rookies," the "kids," the "juniors," but wanting to hear him.

"Why," we wondered aloud, "why is it they all call you . . . the kid?"

He turned, stared drugged and stupid. "Huh," he concentrated uncertainly, mouth hanging open in effort, drooling almost . . . pondering . . . considering . . . remembering faces. "Dunno," he muttered, "dunno, always have, alla' guys in squad . . . alla' guys with the squad are . . . twenty." He stopped, licked filthy lips, continued, "I'm just . . . I ain't," then finished lamely, shyly, "I'm only nineteen yet." We waited. . . . The voice from the paddies came again. The aidman rubbed at his bloody hands.

"Ah . . . balls!" came whispering from beneath scraggly beard as rising slowly, creaking, disjointed, hunchbacked with heavy medical pack and old age he half stumbled, half slid off down the hillside and away from us. He didn't bother to look at the dead boy part way down. Midway he started running. Soon he was gone.

It was still early in the morning; scarcely an hour had passed, but we were very tired.

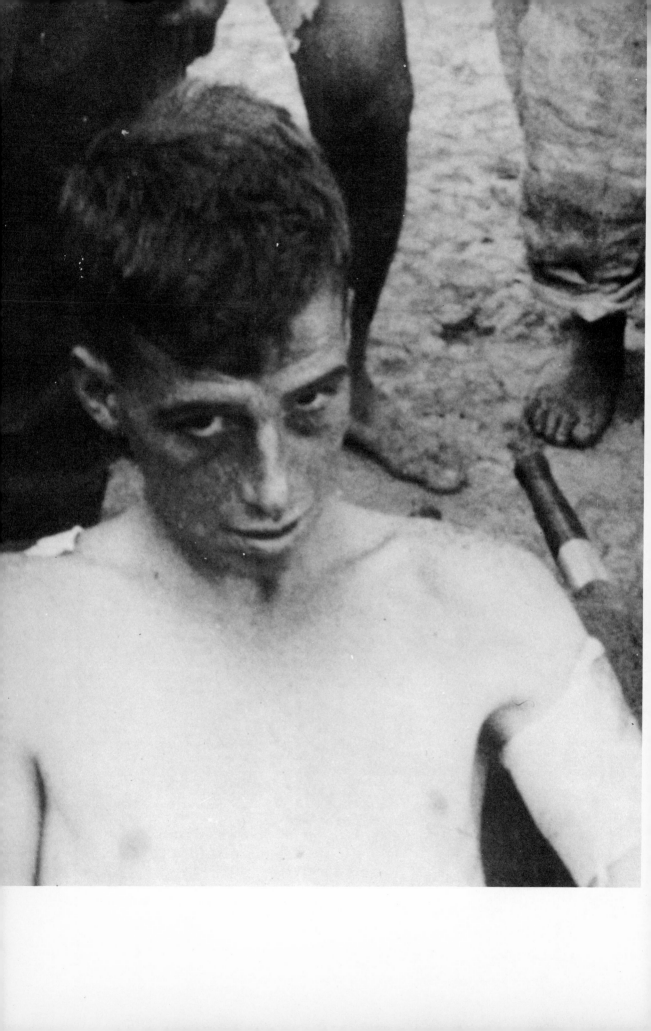

CHAPTER THREE

MASSACRE ON hill 303

IT WAS a picture-book war. For two days we had lain in the sun and watched our air support, jets with rockets, mustangs with fire bombs as they roared low over us, darted across the valley and raked the smoking slope of Hill 303. It was an old sight by now. Riflemen around us scarcely noticed. To the left, the town of Waegwan was afire as usual. Down there two tanks, tiny in the distance, were firing, slamming shells into the reverse slope of 303.

Our units had been pushed off the hill two days previously in the confusion of a dawn attack. Elements of the North Korean forces, crossing the river, had struck from their rear and were in among the scattered companies defending the hill before our people knew it. One unit, the heavy mortar platoon, was known to have been overrun. Some of the mortar men managed to break through. Their survivors dazedly reported.

"They was on us before we could see them . . . They marched up the road just like those gooks we had been lookin' for in support and they hit us."

Confusion had developed because just before dawn the hard-pressed units atop the hill had called for reinforcements. Battalion had informed them by radio that a company of South Koreans were on the

way up. Apparently our people mistook the enemy for their support until it was too late. At least half the platoon had been captured.

In the early afternoon sudden word came down the line.

Scouts had brought in a man from 303. Yes the Reds had captured twenty-six of our men . . . took all their equipment . . . shoes . . . had made them haul ammo and water up and down the hill . . . herded them into a gulley with hands tied behind their backs. Some of the men had cried and screamed. Most had been silent. They were very thirsty. A few scooped with their chins at the sand trying to draw water. It wouldn't work. Then suddenly four Koreans appeared above them. Burp guns had spat fire and staccato reports echoed across the gully stitching bullets up and down the line of helpless Americans.

One of the men who lived through it (there were three who did, we discovered later) was nineteen-year-old Roy Manring, a red-headed pfc from Chicago. He had burrowed under the bodies of his comrades for protection during the shooting. Wounded in each leg and one arm he had managed to crawl down from 303. He was able to talk. As plasma

flowed into him in a company aid station, he gave the halting narrative to unbelieving troopers.

Orders came. A recon patrol was to go out. Attempt to locate the bodies. Do whatever was necessary. It was thought our air had pushed the gooks from the hilltop.

We went up in nine heavily armed jeeps, riflemen clinging as we moved swiftly forward. They were the I & R platoon of the 5th Cavalry Regiment under orders of Lt. Paul Kelly, a daredevil of the Naktong. With us we took Capt. A. M. Kiner of Kiel, Wisconsin, regimental chaplain, who had insisted on coming.

Soon the little column pushed through deserted and burning Waegwan. Pulling vehicles to the roadside, men spread out across the rice paddies, half hidden by the grass fronds as they advanced on the hill. The charred remnants of a house lay on the approaches to the slope. Men in single file jumped across a clay wall deeply shadowed by the overhanging trees of 303.

·Commands were given by hand signal. We became aware of that
weetish odor so familiar in Korea these days.

Ahead came a low call. The lead scout had found two men of the
platoon. They lay with weapons still unslung from their backs, apparently outer guards, killed in the first rush of the action as the platoon
was overrun.

A few feet farther we came to the gully. Everything was as
Manring had said. No one said anything. The boys lay packed tightly,
shoulder to shoulder, lying on their sides, curled like babies sleeping in
the sun. Their feet, bloodied and bare, from walking on the rocks, stuck
out stiffly.

Features were gray-green and waxen. Two in the center had died
with heads turned to the killers, looking directly into the faces of those
guns, lips slitted back in snarls of defiance and teeth gritted tightly.

All had hands tied behind their backs, some with cord, others with
regular issue Army communication wire. Only a few of the hands were

49

clenched. Bullet holes as if put on with black paint, dotted and evenly spaced, crisscrossed the backs.

The place smelled. The air was hot, unshifting, overpowering.

Chaplain Kiner was down in the ditch. He rested on one knee. A small prayerbook fluttered in one hand. His earnest, dusty face regarded the bodies as of some sad-eyed prophet. We heard his voice droning, "Requiescant . . . in . . . pace . . . Amen," the familiar Latin words seeming out of place, unreal.

His hand rose, fell, crossed in the sign of the benediction.

Beside us Kelly stood, hard and bitter, looking down on the gully, hen back to Waegwan smoldering across the paddies.

"Have to get the medics up to get 'em out," he said.

He rubbed the back of his neck. His eyes glanced up and around, larted past us, under the trees, over the field, searching.

"Nothing we can do for 'em now," he repeated.

The chaplain came out of the gully and we started off down the

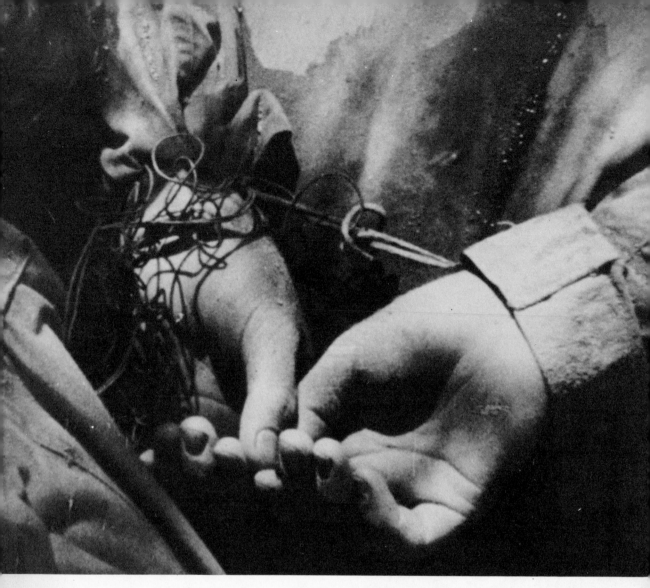

ravine. As we left, the last figure in line, one who had been staring silently at the boys in the ditch turned his back, walked three steps, sat down. His shoulders twisted, he bumped his head up and down savagely on his arm. Words gurgling and liquid came to us.

"Goddam fuggin' bastards . . . ain't human . . . left him all alone . . . fuggin' . . . fuggin' . . . fuggin' . . . bastards." One more figure stopped, went over, caressed the back of the man's neck with a hand. The big BAR hanging on his shoulder slipped to the ground. We could hear him repeating over and over, "Ah Christ, Harry, he ain't alone . . . they're with him."

After a moment the two rose, followed us down the trail. Later on, passing us, he mumbled out of the side of his mouth.

"That Harry . . . recognized the ring on the hand of the Loot . . . used to drive for him back in Jap land."

52

We came to a little glade, the warm afternoon sun slanting through the pine trees. It was a glade of death. All alone, almost casually scattered among the soft pine needles, helmets of the twenty-six lay. Between them, papers, pictures, a few letters drifted in the breeze.

Chaplain Kiner walked about in the little patches of sunbeams and shade. He stooped, picking up the occasional papers. He mused as if talking to himself, as if reciting a sermon of some sort.

"The faces of men and the minds of animals."

We climbed back in the jeeps and headed towards Waegwan where, beyond, the river known as Naktong shimmered peacefully beneath the green hills.

CHAPTER FOUR

RAIN

SEPTEMBER was a wet and bloody month for rifle companies fighting in the hills flanking the "Naktong Line" above Taegu. We were retreating again. No one knew where the support that had been promised was going. The remnants of the same tired divisions which had held off the gooks in midsummer were still facing them alone.

Spirit as well as combat efficiency can always be gauged by the weather when talking of those who fight from their holes in the ground. Wet weather is hell. Clothes rot and rip, rations get tasteless and sodden. Ammo is slippery and fouled. Living in the line is a stupor of slipping, sliding through muddy brambles, water rising in foxholes, always dripping through that one accessible spot on a poncho at the back of the neck to form a gritty damp fabric of its own over the skin. Dry clothes and sleep are a memory that exist only in that fabulous place, the rear area.

The gooks had broken through again, using the heavy mist shrouding the hilltops as a screen from our people in the air.

It rained heavily, almost like a tropical storm in intensity. Going forward in a jeep we skidded from rut to rut, water and mud spraying in a fan from under our wheels. We stopped at a regimental CP. Things looked bad. They had just arrived, retreating from a forward position

up the valley in apparently a hell of a hurry. What few tents were up canted crazily against the gray skyline. Men shivered over communication equipment. In one tent we saw the regimental commander and his staff silently standing about a 300 set. Over the static and the pound of rain we heard dim broken voices from that other land up the road. Lost souls calling to each other, seeking assurances, promises. We heard:

"Baker to Rosemary one . . . they are at the stone wall, give us fire support."

"Fox able to Fox . . . we hear tank motors . . . send . . ."

Then clear, distinct, calm as a church deacon, a metallic voice droned.

". . . yes . . . yes . . . their people are all around on the ridges . . . yes . . . in back us now . . . we got wounded all over up here . . . wait your words . . . yes . . . yes . . . yes . . ."

Garbles, blurred, beseeching out of the static came again.

"Baker to Rosemary one . . . they are at the stone wall . . ."

"Baker to Rosemary one . . . at the stone wall . . . stone wall . . . stonewallstonewall . . ."

The voice rose and fell, wailed away into the distance.

We heard enough and left the silent group gathered around the little radio. Outside our skin prickled as we saw that the extra communication men and command drivers had deployed out on either side of the road. Silent, waiting, seemingly unaware of the rain they looked as if they were searching the mist ahead for some unknown monstrous thing.

The jeep sloshed through the mud. Fifteen minutes later as we neared battalion, firing was loud in our ears. From the bushes by the road a figure jumped, waved, shouted in a fast, rattling sing-song voice.

"Don't go up there . . . tell you it's hell up there . . . they come over that hill . . . blocked the road . . . lots guys bad hurt." Then he was gone.

We slowed, moved ahead with our feet hanging over the side ready to jump and run. Sound racketed down the valley. Coming around a bend in the road we came to the roadblock. A six-by truck lay partially in the ditch, chow cans spilling from its gaping rear, the hot food containers steaming in the rain. We saw none of our people.

Hills made a little bowl, their tops invisible one hundred feet from the road in fast shifting clouds. Winds whistled through the heavy growth alongside the road. The echo of gunfire cracked back and forth and around the hillsides, each report seeming distinct and tremendous in reverberation on the wet air. On the road little mudspouts suddenly leaped up. Something went, "umph-thut," and a blister raised on the hood of the jeep. We jumped, fell, rolled into the ditch. Up the bank . . . hazy . . . hunched in the rain two figures peered at a mist-covered hill. One spoke briefly with his rifle. The other leaned above the stock of his BAR, tensed, watching.

Above the smash of the rifles we could feel, almost hear plainly as if a voice had whispered.

"That's a gook . . . that's ours . . . ours . . . theirs."

The high ripping sound of the enemy guns sounded sharply mounting in crescendo above the heavy bark of our weapons.

We looked about . . . found ourselves in a dim, eerie mist-shrouded place. Sounds, sights, seemed magnified . . . out of all proportion.

In the ditch behind us an animal in the mud, unnoticed till now turned over . . . raised itself to look out over the road . . . then slithered across to the wrecked truck. We saw the soldier on his knees at one of the chow cans. He whipped a canteen cup from somewhere beneath sagging coat, dipped it into the can . . . in the same motion, crammed things into his mouth. All around the truck the little mudspouts disputed his right to the food. In seconds he was back in the ditch. He lay on his back, food dribbling from his wet beard, canteen cup clutched possessively in both hands, up against his chest. Head turning from side to side we glimpsed his face, eyes peering furtively each way like a trapped animal. Heard him muttering above the rain, "Mother fuggin' bastards . . . starve me . . . hell."

On the ridge in front of us something wailed up and up saying, "Ohow . . . ohow . . . shhhheeee . . . ohow."

62

We heard rustling in the bushes. Three figures became visible . . . paused in a stoop at the fringe of wet foliage. They mumbled uncertainly to each other, twisted their heads back and forth in quick, jerky motions. Eyeballs gleamed whitely in deep helmets and then barely glancing at us . . . they trotted off down the road.

One spoke over his shoulder as if telling himself something, "Gooks . . . ridge up there . . . overrun us . . . bringing out guy now . . . hurt."

Moments later more riflemen ran from the undergrowth. They seemed nearly bent double as with great weights . . . mouths worked for words that would not come. All seemed to be straining . . . pushing against something. They, too, scampered off down the road.

The reports of the rifles were closing in from all sides now. More figures crashed out of the bushes. Two men supporting a third stumbled over the ditch. In the center we saw momentarily . . . an old-young face . . . alabaster white, pale freckles standing out like nail heads

. . . fingers clawing to hold the flesh of his cheek in place . . . hands pressed tightly . . . blood shockingly scarlet seeping through his fingers . . . eyes pain-filled, staring out at us. He sang, "Ohow . . . uhu . . . ohow . . ." crooned gurgling vomiting noises to himself.

They shambled off down the road oblivious to the rifle fire echoing in on them, their feet making sucking clinging noises in the mud as the wind pulled at their clothes.

Behind them, sodden blanket whipping from his shoulders, one more came, paused . . . watched them go off down the road and disappear around the bend. We could see his mouth moving . . . rain jerking the words from his lips . . . heard vaguely, "Told 'em . . . knew gooks . . . hit the stonewall . . . told 'em . . . told 'em . . . told 'em damit."

He dropped into the ditch, lay back tiredly. Head turned towards us. Flat pinched face peering from beneath his muddy helmet . . . eyes hooded, secretive, licking his lips. Looked at the sky . . . spat . . . said to no one as we crawled off down the ditch, "Hear they're gonna try a end run . . . Christ, better try somethin' . . . said the Marines was carrying the ball . . . seaport . . ."

Then weak, disinterested over his shoulder . . . looking to the ridge, "Inchon . . . yeah . . . said they call the place Inchon."

seawall at blue beach

THEY had called for the pros. Specialists in amphibious assaults. The Marine Corps.

It was like old times. Five years dropped away at a first glance. Gray skies . . . big transports like massive elephants of the seas . . . hundreds of tiny landing craft . . . Marines climbing down cargo nets. In the distance . . . gunfire . . . smoke . . . flames seen dimly. Water littered with floating debris.

The five days aboard the transport from the staging area of Japan had gone swiftly. D-Day was to be different from others in that the main landing force would not go ashore until 5:00 P.M., one hour before dusk closed in. A treacherous tide could only then cover the mud-flats that rested in the outer approaches to the beaches.

The amtrac wallowed, dipped, moved sluggishly circling near the control boat. From the driver's compartment a big stick, square-boxed sign on its top, hung above us. The numbers 2–2 stood out plainly. Numbers that identified us as the second amtrac in the second wave, assaulting a seawall fronting that unknown place ahead designated merely as "Blue Beach One." We were to hit the wall thirty seconds after the first Marines moved over.

It felt good. There is something powerful, massive, coordinated in amphibious assault.

Ahead loomed the big control boat. It seemed the size of a destroyer. Every turret, mast and even the sides, were forested with radio aerials. At intervals along its deck drifted sentinels in denim blue, heads buried in deep communication helmets, radiophones hanging from their chests, controllers for the assault waves. On the stern a gun crew grouped around a 5-inch rifle . . . threw things into metal compartments . . . moved clicking doors . . . sent shells slamming out flat trajectory fire into the haze.

Tempo of the firing stepped up. We moved to one side of the amtrac, peered into the smoke that hung over the water, masking the distance. Judged ourselves to be about a mile off the seawall. The faces of the Marines were static . . . expressionless . . . almost disinterested. They were pros. People who accepted the routine of direct frontal assault upon a defended shoreline as calmly as walking down a drill field. Hard people. Men rode these boats who had crawled across every hot beach from Tarawa to Iwo in the Pacific campaigns. Even the youngsters had the easy look of veterans. This was a platoon from the

famed First Marines who in this war had taken casualties, fought fiercely, left their dead thickly in the hills surrounding the Pusan perimeter.

Ahead rockets wooshed up above the smoke, hurried back down in graceful arching power. They made a continuous curtain of steel. We couldn't see the little ships but knew they were in there trying to soften it up for us. Suddenly, to our front, moving in column, three destroyers appeared. Steaming parallel to us they moved slowly past, all guns firing. First one turret then another, raking across the water, seeking out the invisible shoreline with red pencil lines of steel. They slipped into the haze to our left. Minutes later came back on the return journey. Now there was no separation to the sound of their guns. No deferential bowing of one turret to another. The air was a solid roar of explosions. Faintly, odd-sounding and high above the noise, we could hear the tat-tat-tatatatatatat of smaller weapons. The people on those tin cans must have been firing even their machine guns, over the handrails.

Far to our flanks and behind us we saw bigger flashes. Big cruisers and other ships of the fleet all over the horizon were throwing shells to our front.

Planes in a canopy bored in low. Their winking machine guns seemed pointing right at us as they swept over at tree-top height level-

ing off into the obscurity ahead. Corsairs, piloted by brother Marines. Well-trained and expert. The closest air-infantry support in existence.

A Marine, baseball cap looking out of place on the back of his head, leaned from the driver's compartment.

"Got the word . . . going in," he shouted above the roar of our motors.

The long circle opened up, the amtrac ahead leading us onward in a slow bobbing line over the swells.

Control boat slipped past . . . talkers on the deck stared over us . . . unseeing . . . mouths moving . . . speaking unheard confidences into mouthpieces on their chests. One, probably our wave controller, ran a few steps down the railing. Hands megaphoned to his mouth, then he dropped them without speaking. Grinned widely. Fist clenched . . . arm pumped up and down . . . we moved rapidly past him. A Marine moved to the side of the amtrac, stood on tiptoe. His hand raised slowly, carefully. Put thumb to his nose, fingers waving a majestic farewell as the control boat slipped past.

The men about me began performing a busy, hurried ritual. Dropping life belts . . . shrugging on packs . . . slapping at their rifles.

"Aw right . . . load and lock," sang back over the shoulder of the Marine standing on the firing parapet of the bow machine gun. His

hand rested on the gun shield. We caught a quick, momentary vision
of some hills, flames burning brightly on their slopes, then the dark
vaporous clouds closed in again. We seemed to be running parallel to
the coast. In the amtrac, people were pulling at cardboard containers,
passing egg-like cylinders out to reaching hands. Rings on their ends
gleamed softly. Fingers hung them on belts, through collar loops.
Bayonets rasped up out of scabbards, clicked faintly on the metal of

rifle barrels.

"You goddam people," a voice grumbled.

"Won't you never learn to tape your grenades . . . you're gonna kill yourselves that way someday," it went on.

He sat leaning against the steel plates at the stern. Bare-headed, curly black hair wet from the spray, speaking around a cig dangling from the corner of his lips. Earphones, mouthpiece and communication wire collared his neck. A corporal, a forward com man, he seemed in charge of the men. A few pulled tape off the containers, wrapped it around the rings, rehung them. In a corner two voices rose, one plaintively, querulously.

". . . tell you is so . . . goddamit you always get the extra one inna case . . ." it argued. Then continued, wheedling, demanding, ". . . ain't right now . . . my turn tell ya' . . . gimme it now . . . my turn tell ya'."

People in the center moved apart, caught a glimpse of two figures, dress, faces, twin-like. One held his palm up. The other, straightened . . . mumbled.

". . . ah, shitass . . ." plucked something from his belt . . . plunked a grenade down in a waiting hand . . . turned his back, hand cupped his chin, staring out over the steel side. The other smugly, carefully, as one who hoards jewels, slid the object of affection between the buttons of his blouse, happy, satisfied.

Watching them, hearing their talk, thinking their thoughts, it felt good. Only such in the Marines. It would have seemed unsafe, improper to make this journey in other than their company.

Motors slowed, idled. The column swinging, turning into a wave line abreast of each other. From the driver's compartment of each rose a silhouette, shadowy arms raised palms one behind the other in signal. Down the line one gesticulated in a fast abrupt motion, waved in towards the brown smoke smudging up over the water. Our silhouette stooped, peered anxiously around from the protection of the gunshield. Motors ripped up in a crescendo. The wave had reached the line of departure. We crossed over. Haze, smoke, sound closed in on us. Almost immediately the amtracs on either side, only fifty feet away, were shrouded, invisible. We were moving in a conelike vacuum down which we seemed to be rushing, rocking on a railroad track of motion. Ahead great unknown voices coughed, thumped, wailed up into the gloom. Things happened fast. A face turned from the hatch in our bow. Swift, racing words on top of each other.

71

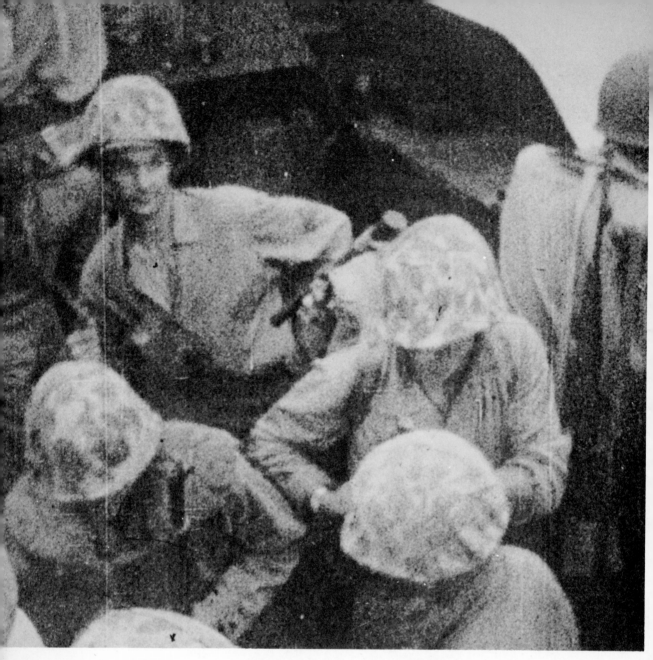

"... first wave ... just ahead ... mixup ... gonna hafta hit it with their people ... ," it said.

Around me men got to one knee. Heads, eyes intent on the steel rivets in the deck fronting us. No emotion. No feeling. This was the place. "Pick up your brass, secure the butts, and move out mister."

The air talked to itself. Things plopped into the water around us, spouts rose, gesticulated, danced hand in hand in the spray. They went, "... umph ... thut ... thupthut ..." and caromed off into disgusted nothingness.

At our bow the 50cal spoke fluently, addressing their passing. We looked up over the edge. A magic hand was raising the curtain. The

seawall, high-jutting rocks, closely packed, came up. Like water bugs swimming madly in the confusion of an upheaval, amtracs were moving just in front and to our sides. They circled, floundered, rose and fell, bounced off the wall. Men crouched behind the shields, firing every which way over the stones rising ahead. Two of the water bugs moved in, butted against the obstruction. Figures jumped on the tractor treads on either side. One jumped . . . moved rapidly up and over, turned . . . arms out as if reaching for something. Two others started up. One lifted his foot. An invisible man swatted him with a ball bat. He jerked, sagged forward, his feet spun up, his body rolled over the wall. The other, hit too, leaned against the reaching one, slid back on the amtrac treads. We ducked back onto the steel bottom, heard shouts, fast rattling of machine gun fire . . . sensed rather than saw the others out there going up and over.

"Make for the hole in the wall," curly-head yelled, rising, pointing to a place where shellfire had gouged out a gaping hole in the seawall.

We felt the amtrac surge forward, bounce off the steel side of another one . . . the wall loomed suddenly, huge above us. We slammed into the stones, slid a few feet, could see a strange place through the entrance naval guns had prepared for our arrival. Gritted rocky turf, twisted debris . . . a few feet ahead and to the right a sandbagged gun pit . . . tin roof gashed and ripped askew. Sudden action. The man nearest the bow, hunched swiftly forward on one knee, jumped upright to the steel plates. Hand swung back, carbine outthrust in the other, threw, dropped flat, as the grenade exploded. Then up again as if rehearsed. Moving up fast, low, weaving, running inland through the smoke and dust. The first rifleman. A man to know. We followed him. Plopped into the dugout. It was empty, still smelling of cordite from the grenade. Behind us stones rattled. The amtrac backed out. Voices yelled.

". . . down to the boat basin . . . can get over there . . . back with you in a minute." Then they were gone.

The tractors were to stay with us the first night. Apparently had found a way of crawling ashore over the debris of the boat basin, a half mile down the seawall where other Marines were moving in.

We lay in the dugout. Around us twisted, jagged rails and pieces of rusted machinery humped grotesquely amid the debris. Slugs ricocheting off produced a constant whining noise. Behind us Marines were torrenting over the seawall, rolling, falling, clutching weapons to their chests. Boxes, water cans, a heavy mortar tube came sailing up out of nowhere. Unseen hands pitching them over in a hasty deluge.

The littered flatness behind the wall was crowded with obscure indistinct objects, vague fast-moving shadows that crawled about on hands and knees. Their talk bawled loudly amid the sharp reports of machine gun fire. They babbled among themselves . . .

". . . where's battalion . . . want to know . . . CP against those ruins . . . guess . . . corpsmen in on the fifth wave the man said . . . come the 'tracs . . ."

Mortar bursts were raining in on us now. It moved up from the water, reaching out among the crawling figures. Lifted stones, sprayed debris, threw people from the wall. Flung them down into the darkness. It seemed light, about 60mm size. The shrapnel thudded into the rails around us, ate at the sandbags. Small arms whispered in the air. Felt you could cup a palm, reach up, grab a handful, easily.

Down the wall a flat, dry voice intoned . . . repeated itself . . . "Yellow jacket to Fox five . . . 3rd battalion over the wall . . . receiv-

ing mortar and small arms . . . moving inland . . . authority Big Jack . . ."

Tall aerial swayed on the com man's back, weighted and bulky with a 300 set as he rose, trudged off behind a small chesty man who walked bent forward, peering to left and right in the murk.

Our amtrac was up. Marines sliding to either side as the big treads chewed past. Ahead bobbed the baseball cap, its wearer trotting . . . .45 in one hand. He shouted things over his shoulder to it, waved imperiously, pointed directions, pounded once on the steel hatch in anger. He disappeared down the seawall, the big vehicle jerking, lumbering on behind, the 50cal over the guide's head spitting out protection like some great dog growling over a tiny mastif.

Around us voices welled up, "Move out . . . man says to . . . move out . . ." they cried.

About thirty minutes had passed since we came over the wall. It was getting dark fast. Behind us, the blood-red ball of the sun rested flatly on the sea.

We took off in sprints, running, crouching, dropping to one knee, running, again falling in holes or among the rails and rockpiles. Up ahead, seen dimly against the flames that were Inchon we saw the blurred shifting shadows of other Marines. Their bayonets moved forward in the twilight.

CHAPTER SIX

THE ROAD TO SEOUL

THE main objective of our end run up the coast was Seoul, traditional capital of Korea and queen city of the free Republic. A vital road and rail junction, its seizure would put new life into an almost defeated people and place our arms in position to launch an offensive towards the north.

Between Inchon and Seoul lay the river Han. Sluggish and wide, it formed a natural barrier which must be bridged.

The dawn crossing was uneventful. First waves went over in amtracs, supporting units following in amphibious ducks.

On the other side long columns of the 1st Marine Division formed up, wound snakelike across the grassy fields towards the hills before the road to Seoul.

The first day we drew occasional sniper fire. Artillery only in the afternoon. Every third round was white phosphorus. Bad stuff. Not much noise, just a dull thump, then a large dirty cloud of white smoke rising up. It burns into the flesh and is almost impossible to extinguish.

At night we dug in with the first hills looming up ahead. Tanks faced in every direction, covering us, much in the manner of an old-time wagon train, circled for defense from all sides. This was beginning to be a cowboy-Indian kind of warfare in the open country.

Dew was heavy and it got cold soon after the sun went down. A chill wind slipped down from the slopes. In the holes at night, covered only by damp earth, it is like trying to sleep in a deep-freeze box. You never really sleep, just doze. The mind is just going blank when earth trickles down your neck, the cold or gunfire jars you awake. It gets colder. You try to curl up in a ball. Half an hour of this and your legs go numb. The position cramps your stomach. So all night it's curl, uncurl, freeze, doze, and wish to God the sun would come up.

At dawn, dressing is the simple act of putting on a helmet as you climb out of the ground (here you sleep fully clothed, including boots). Breakfast is crackers and coffee. Your stove, an empty C ration can filled

with a half inch of borrowed gasoline from the jeep. Throw in a handful of dirt, bend the edge in on either side for ventilation, and drop in a match. Put on top a canteen cup filled with brew and in two minutes you have your morning cup of steaming java, style à la infantry.

Giants began to slam doors far away in the distance and seconds later the morning's outgoing mail rumbled overhead. They are putting up an artillery preparation for the jump-off.

Up forward a Marine rises, waves his platoon out. Their figures bulky, encumbered, loom large as they crowd over the skyline accompanied by the sputtering discordance of small arms fire.

Near the top, a long line of support column winds along. A rifle speaks harshly from their flank. One man is down from the sniper. We see him lying on the trail, bright blood oozing from a dark hole in his neck, jetting forth regularly with his breaths. A corpsman is on his knees beside the still figure. Marines move around him, stepping quickly over his rifle lying in the path where it had fallen.

From the ridge we watched a company fan out . . . small ant-like figures moving forward across the open field below. An officer sitting in the OP nearby reported their progress by radio to regiment. His voice was cynical and battle-worn. He spoke into his hand mike, ". . . moving forward . . . judge they will be in a fire fight in a few minutes . . . probably pinned down."

Still the ants moved forward against the silent enemy. One platoon was half way across the plow furrows. Then it came. We couldn't hear

because of the distance, but all through the ranks of the advancing ants dust spurted. Three fell . . . others ran crouched to fall in the irrigation ditch beside the field. Moments later a lone figure, probably a corpsman, ran from his ditch. Midway the dust jumped demandingly around his feet . . . he tripped . . . fell.

The observer said briefly to his mike, "They are pinned down now."

Artillery support was called for to work on the ground to our front, and under its shelter of steel the rest of the ants straggled back. Four specks of green remained against the brown of the field.

They tried flanking the open space, moving alongside a copse of underbrush. Some made it across. Some didn't. They drew tank fire. We heard it bursting loud in our ears, the wham-whoooom of the projectiles tearing the air in a continuous sound from muzzle blast to explosion. Straight trajectory fire is easily recognizable.

Squeaks came from the radio set and a calm voice from the safety of regiment requested if we had noticed any enemy tank activity.

"Stand by for a message," said the observer, holding the phone in the air, pointing down at the plain below. Soon there was a buzz in the distance. Air had arrived and went to work on the hidden tanks.

We watched them bring in their wounded. Ponchos served as

stretchers. They seemed running straight for us, heads lowered in determination . . . mouths straining . . . they labored forward as the dust puffs again tugged demandingly around them . . . We saw none hit. Seemingly in seconds they were nearing us, then suddenly swerving sideways and then gone over the ridge line.

We crossed over . . . crawled up one more hill. Before us lay Seoul, its veiled rooftops glimmering vaguely in the late afternoon sun. All about us men were setting up observation and command posts, whispering into radios, training their glasses downward as shells crashed into the outskirts of the city. Tomorrow we would go in.

By early morning we were well in the suburbs. At first we drew little resistance. Marines crouched in backyards, firing over fences. Ahead on Mapo Boulevard, the main thoroughfare, the "point" moved forward cautiously. They were the lead. Sent to make contact with the enemy. The three constantly turned about, looking everywhere, prob-

ing, feeling out the unknown ahead for the rest of us.

Suddenly rifle fire cracked down from a building on a little rise to our right. Men scattered. Began to trot forward into the smoke drifting up from the burning city. As the slugs whined off the cement, Marines sprinted forward, heavy packs twisting and jumping up and down. Smoke obscured some of them.

We crossed an alley . . . saw tiny figures running down a side street parallel to us and only a block away. First sight of the enemy. At a run all Marines crossing fired down the brick defile.

On the other side they bunched up, smoke whirling up in back of them. Many began coughing. Slugs whipped into the pavement where some had been sitting, taking a breather. The riflemen jumped in every direction yelling and bringing up their weapons. One ran to the other side of the street . . . paused beside a sewer opening . . . whipped a grenade from his belt . . . His hand reared back and we heard the dull thump of the explosion underground. Moments later we had taken our first prisoner. Dazed, bleeding from concussion, he crawled out with arms upraised. A bend in the sewage pipe had saved him from shrapnel.

By now the sidewalk was packed as if in a pre-Christmas rush back home. Here, however, the shoppers wore steel hats, their old clothes and carried guns. The whole battalion was moving up in mass. Assault companies moved out at a dead run, the men spaced at twenty-foot intervals, bobbing and weaving, sinking to the street as soon as they stopped. As fast as they were chopped up, other companies filtered through to take their place on the point. It was a fast-moving, efficient method of attack.

The battle of the barricades began. We found a barrier of earth-filled rice bags shoulder-high and stretching across the street, barring our way from wall to wall. A bazooka team ran forward to blast a hole for us. The noise was terrific. The air was filled with whining, shrieking sounds. The two ran for a few feet to our front . . . dropped to one knee. The loader placed the projectile in the rear of the tube . . . tapped the crouching gunner on the shoulder and leaned away. We waited. A loud wooosh-wham followed instantly—too soon. The rocket struck and was detonated by a heavy power cable dangling thirty feet in front of us. At the blast, shrapnel rattled off our pavement. A Marine, lying prone in the debris littering the street, stared sullenly at the bazookaman, spat out his words, "Christ sake . . . dumb bastard . . . could get killed around here."

The man ahead with the big tube threw another round forward,

and as the dust lifted we saw our door had been opened.

The assault company spent the night behind that barricade. Fires made the streets daylight bright and all night gunfire echoed up and down Mapo Boulevard.

At dawn they moved out again . . . soon crossed another barricade in much the same manner as before.

"There you go," a voice yelled. We looked up on our right . . . saw fifty to sixty tiny figures, small in the distance, running up a side street. They disappeared into a large building, the top floors of which were already afire. Soon our side of the street visible to them was receiving their fire. Support units bunched up behind us. We were

pinned down. The company CO ordered everyone to the unexposed side of the avenue. Carying a walkie-talkie cradled in his arms, he muttered into it as he ran back with us.

In a few minutes we felt the pavement begin to shake as five heavy tanks mounting 90mm's rolled up and through the barricade. Shells ripped up the street, bricks sailed out and portions crumbled. Soon clouds of dust and smoke obscured the buildings, but the tanks kept firing. The Marines lolled on the safe side of the street, protected by the heavy walls. Canteens, rations, and smokes came out. Some catnapped, leaning back on the packs, using them as pillows. Some even wrote letters. Others just day-dreamed, staring blankly at walls across the

93

street. They were only six feet away from death. Pros, hardened and able to take their leisure where they could find it.

We looked to our rear. They had not been so lucky. Snipers had let the point pass and then opened up on the support from side streets and buildings. Every hundred feet or so a Marine lay, a corpsman usually crouched beside him. Only the dead had no helper.

We crawled back to a corner where a collecting station had been set up. Wounded lay spread about the sidewalk. Against the wall, his head in the lap of a buddy, lay a corpsman, shot through the knee while going to the aid of a fallen Marine. At times, more from grief than pain, all men will cry . . . even Marines.

Further down a Marine dashed across to a still figure on the far sidewalk. He picked up a rifle, snatched something from around the

limp sacklike waist. He puffed up, addressing men in the aid station. I
his hand he carried a pearl-handled six-shooter.

"Simpson got it through the head . . . get the Gunny to send th
to his folks in Bridgeport will ya'." He threw it at us and was off dow
the street and into the smoke. The revolver lay on the sidewalk unt
a corpsman stuck it in the waistband of his dungarees.

Around us the air still talked to itself in guttural mumbles, shriek

and whispers. Through the noise we heard the flat tone-deadened words of the casualties as they flowed back:

"Yeah the loot got it bad . . . inna guts . . . Baker Company having troubles . . . big doings with that gook hotel . . . tol' him he better carry that one more bandoleer . . . you know eightball, he knows everything."

They started trying to get the wounded out. Stretchers were at a

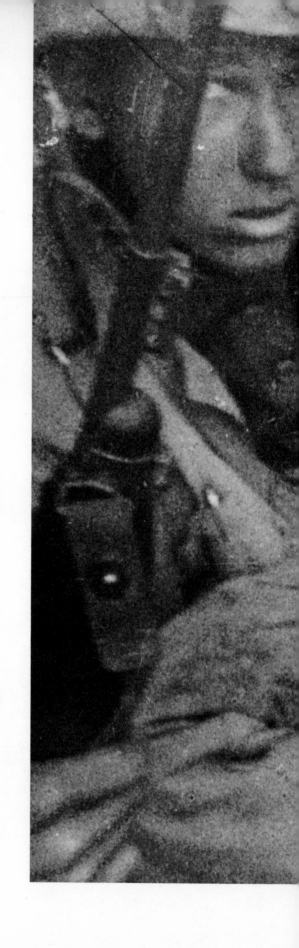

premium in Seoul, so wooden doors were dragged from the wreckage
and pressed into service. Four men at a time trotting at a crouch back
down the avenue. Bodies rolling on the woodwork, blood dripping,
staining the white powder of the roadway. Walking wounded followed
them.

The day passed and again the assault units spent the night against
the barricades. Another day, another fire, blocks gained.

Next morning we moved into the downtown business section. At
the barricades we now were receiving fire from flanking buildings. Men
ran into the nearest, shouting wildly. A tank rumbled up ahead, moved
in close, the big gun actually jutting through a window. The foundation
shook, shifted, settled, the tank backed out smugly, white debris
covering the barrel and turret. Further up two tanks, bulldozer blades
in front, raked their machine guns up and down the sidewalks and into
the doorways. In return we could hear a harvest of slugs banging off the

steel blades like rain drops hitting a tin roof. Marines fired, ran about, threw grenades into windows, sewers, down cellars and across the barricades. They crouched . . . whirled . . . threw up rifles . . . snarled . . . slitted eyes . . . squeezed triggers.

Again on our right figures moved. Marines screamed and opened fire. Several minutes later a panting, cursing man ran in and announced in heated tones, "You bastards are shooting up the second battalion— knock it off." He conferred with the company CO . . . a map was brought out . . . the profane one made pointing, demanding gestures with his arms. The firing on the hill to the left was stopped. The runner sprinted away, appeased by our awareness of the second battalion.

To the front, on the point, a rifleman, string-bean long, gangly legs spraddled, lay flush in the gutter, near a sewer opening, peered ahead. He acted as if the six inches of concrete curbing would shield him from all harm. Evidently considered himself a sentry of sorts. Kept raising up

on elbows, probing the smoke ahead with short jerky neck motions as a turtle looks out from its shell. Disrupted his inspection to whip head back over shoulder, whine out, "pahty of fouah comin' down the drag, suh," this to the barricade where the figure of a platoon leader could be seen as he crouched, held fishpole aerial overhead, spoke loving words into a walkie-talkie. The turtle stared, cupped knobby hands to cheeks, yowled again, "people comin' heah . . . you heah me?" The platoon leader looked up, pained, obviously busy, apparently had been conducting a meeting of the executive board with other vice presidents of the concern from different departments down the street, hearing their reports, discussing things of importance, of world-shaking seriousness. Ugly rumor had it battalion was out of frag grenades. If true, business would slip. He must know. He nodded his head quickly to the

105

turtle, resumed his discussion with the invisible others on the com net. The rifleman bobbed his head back, bulked shoulders, looked ahead again. Three men moving fast, quiet, at a semi-crouch, came in out of the smoke and noise. A point, they were those from a recon sent up a side street earlier in the day, after which there had been sudden disturbance, racket of gunfire, yells, catcalls, whistles even. It was felt by the wise ones back of the barricade that they had been taken. As they came closer the turtle-headed rifleman leaped up, ran waving his arms in happy excited little circles of joy, almost sexual pleasure in his wiggling body, kept saying, "Monk . . . Monk, why ain't you dead yet, Monk!" Repeated, "We heard it and knew you was dead, Monk . . . Christ . . . Cain't kill the ape, can they, boy?" He passed the platoon leader who looked up again, said nothing. He walked off down the avenue, staying close, hugging a shattered wall, slapping an arm up and down across a shoulder of the squat dark BAR man who trudged unspeaking and downcast between two taller riflemen. You had to look

close, almost couldn't see the tear stains glistening on the grimy cheeks as they stared at each other. Maybe they were merely sweat streaks. Nobody at the barricade paid them any heed.

We crouched against the rice bags. Suddenly, out of nowhere two men appeared. Wearing communist helmet, black civilian overcoats, blanket rolls over their shoulders and carrying ancient muskets, they peeped over our barricade. We spied them at the same time they saw us. Like open-mouthed tourists they gasped stupidly and we stared back at them just as surprised. Stunned, no one opened fire as we wondered if they were commies or local representatives of the Seoul forces of the interior taking advantage of the open season on Reds. They quickly ducked their heads back and in a moment vanished. We never saw them again or knew who or what they were. Just two travelers in a strange place on a mission of their own.

Several Marines stood up and soon so did we. Looking behind us, a Marine yelled and, turning around, we saw still more visitors ap-

107

proaching down a side street. Forty to fifty gooks, five abreast, all dressed in the dirty brown of North Korea. With no weapons showing, they moved towards us. A single Marine threw his rifle over the parapet and fired into them at about fifty feet. An officer screamed "let 'em come in," but no one paid heed. For now we all could see as the front ranks began to fall, raked from our fire, that those in the center had been carrying an anti-tank gun. It was slaughter at pointblank range. In seconds dust and smoke boiled up around the heaped bodies. None appeared to have escaped. Marines kept firing low into the haze for minutes afterwards, searching for survivors.

A lot of civilians were getting winged. Most were head wounds. These people sometimes hardly seemed aware that war played a bloody game in their front yards. Periodically some citizen, curious, or just stupid, would peep out from a window or inch around a corner. Almost invariably, unavoidably a trigger-quick Marine would wang away, blast them. Whenever possible, aidmen treated them. At one intersection, bordered by a burning brick house, two women and a man darted from the rubble and across the flank of an assault platoon moving up the boulevard. Almost immediately they were cut down. Line people don't like strangers moving sudden and unannounced on their flanks. Waiting at curbside for the jump-off towards the next barricade a block up the avenue, there was time for the platoon corpsmen to treat the Koreans. One of the women was shot in the stomach. The others injured only lightly. Marines dragged the stomach case to a doorway, grouped around as two corpsmen began to examine the wound. The other woman trotted off down the street, her rubber sandals making flat slapping fear-filled sounds of haste. The man dropped to one knee, watching as the woman lay back, semiconscious, making frightened cooing little bleats of pain. Whimpering. An inch above and to the right of her navel a little dark hole poked inward, oozed bright blood. Marines stared expressionlessly.

"She don't know it, but she's dead five minutes ago," said one of the corpsmen as he daubed canteen water on aid packet, sprinkled sulfa powder, injected morphine from syrette in all the routine places for wound, gunshot, abdominal. The other aidman supported her shoulder, kept pushing away the ineffectual, fumbling, pleading hands of the Korean man. Perhaps her husband. His lips moved wordlessly, beady eyes followed every gesture of the treatment. Sweat and dust filth crowned his clipped head in a skullcap of despair. The corpsmen of the hurrying hands looked up, asked, "Ain't bad-looking tail for a gook

broad, huh?" to audience of watching riflemen. He was a kind man and very weary. Living only, perhaps, on the cigar butt which jutted from yellowed teeth and the ritual of sticking his hands into the gaping wounds of his Marines.

One of the helmeted watchers scratched chest, armpits, requested of another, "Gimme a butt," inquired of the aid group, "what would you

do for a pro . . . and the stink to 'em . . . that kumchee crap they eat."

The corpsman continued at his work, deft hands busy, mumbled around the cigar, "DDT my boy . . . DDT . . . God's answer to Korean women," winked knowingly, eyes filled with pretended experience.

The questioneer stared long, casually flicked dust from rifle, answered, "It ain't worth it . . . I ain't that hard up for tail . . . yet." Heard low above the noise of combat came a racking, wheezing sound of breathing as in the nose. This from the woman who began to vibrate, tremble as the wheezing came faster.

"Aw screw it . . . long gone . . . long gone," said the aidman as he and his buddy gently laid the still gasping woman flat.

"Skipper . . . this gook'll croak in a minute . . . nothin' now," said the other to one who peered with binoculars over the barricade ahead.

He answered only, "Aw right . . . you people . . . move out," started waving his arm in a side-level gesture of command down the street as the platoon moved forward in assault. The querying rifleman ran bobbing, and directly behind the learned corpsman. Words filtered back.

"DDT tell you . . . broads love the stuff, boy," and rallying up came the familiar cry of the rifle troops, all inclusive, a battle cry, "fug 'em . . . fug 'em all," as the smog and gunfire of Mapo swallowed them up. The Korean man lay down beside the woman. He drew her close to him.

Support companies moved by.

A bearded Marine gunnery sergeant came up. Behind him a single small South Korean civilian trotted. The man wore a goatee and carried a large American flag wrapped tight about a six-foot wooden staff. He peered fearfully over the barricade.

The Gunny casually crouched. Talked mildly, pronounced his words evenly, turned his head from side to side surveying the scene as one long used to inhabiting such places. As one who has found both a home and occupation therein. A mustache, cavalry style, drooped below a hawk nose and his mottled helmet cover hung loosely back across his neck. The massed chevrons of his rank, seen rarely on Marine dungarees, stood out clearly. A bayoneted rifle swung over one shoulder. His voice rambled on . . . telling of how the CO was having him do everything and anything . . . how he had to get up the rations . . .

watch the ammo . . . keep his people warm at night . . . worry over them.

A young Marine nearby took up the joke, asking "Is the smoking lamp lit, Gunny?"

The sergeant looked at him, smiled thinly, said, "Sure is, chicken . . . just point out the building you want and I'll burn it down personal for a lighter . . . one more day now and we'll all be smoking under the capitol dome."

Then he announced he had to hurry off to reserve a room in a burning hotel down the street. His flag bearer followed behind, little legs pumping to keep up with the strides of the big leatherneck.

Far up the avenue seen dimly in the smoke were tiny figures with bayonets on their rifles. The point moved forward for the final assault. They dashed back and forth, weaving amid the flaming buildings and littered streets. Little men out on the rim of nowhere, moving at their work in a smoking land between two worlds. . . . The sound of Seoul was loud in our ears.

streetfighter

SEOUL was nearly ours. The streetfighters of the 1st Marine Division had pushed their bayonets forward through the rubble for four days, fighting a battle of the barricades.

We came to the last barrier and still Seoul flamed, rocked and shook in the throes of her rebirth. Riflemen paused momentarily.

War to us is in memory merely a series of related sequences as if photographed on the brain for all time. Sometimes the pattern is hazy, confused. Sometimes in the faces that come up, feelings . . . smells . . . and the mood can be brought back in a second.

We looked around us. There was a man. A big man. He slouched nearby, on one knee . . . resting. He wore ragged dungarees. On his arm were the inked chevrons of a corporal, and over his heart the faded badge of the Marine Corps. A field pack raised his back . . . bayoneted carbine cradled easily in one arm . . .

A full face . . . bearded . . . blackened with the crust of battle. Wide helmet with the familiar camouflage covering . . . sitting as if its owner had been born with it on. He turned towards us . . . eyeballs gleaming . . . tongue wetting lips . . .

Remote, fleeting expressions of concentration . . . decision . . . Ready now

. . . calling behind the barricades . . . for orders . . . "move out in 30 seconds" . . .

thinking perhaps . . . "they ain't playing with marbles out there."

. . . grenade adjusted for a collar ornament . . . looking ahead into a smoky future . . .

A moment's pause . . .

and the Marine Corps is moving up . . . a human lance, tipped with steel . . . as

the corporal rises . . . takes his squad out . . . a tired, harried busi-
nessman

. . hurrying forward . . . keeping an urgent appointment up the street.

CHAPTER EIGHT

AIRBORNE ASSAULT

THE Angels From Hell were impatient. For a month paratroopers of the 187th Airborne Regiment had been waiting on the flat plain before Seoul. Kept apart from others. Penned in a huge barbed wire enclosure of mudholes and ramshackle barracks a mile across from Kempo airport. In their cage the animals of the Airborne were irritable, fretted, peered sullenly out at Kempo, wondered profanely if they would be allowed to perform on this stage that was Korea.

Rumors, the little old women of words, were their only visitors. Day and night the paratroopers argued . . . and cajoled.

". . . Marine Corps won't let 'em use us . . . send us to Jap land for guard duty . . . not enough parachutes . . . place called Sukchon . . . straight dope I tell ya'."

It was the straight dope. The word had come down: Plan "A" was to go into effect at 2200 hours on the . . . th. The drop zone would be a valley, thirty-five miles above Pyongyang. Regimental headquarters, the 1st and 3rd battalions were to jump at Sukchon, the 2nd battalion going in twelve miles to the west at Sunchon.

The single road of escape from the enemy capital split at a junction point, wound through these places going north. The regiment had a dual mission. They were to fan out, seize the hills, block off retreating

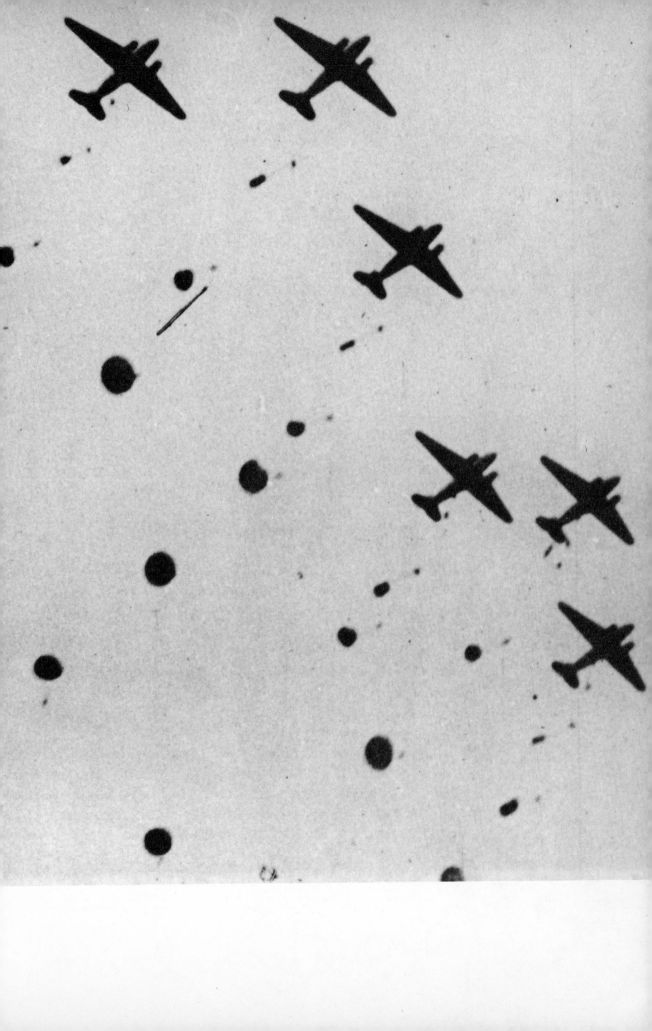

Reds. Intelligence said the enemy herded 4500 of our people before them, prisoners taken during the summer. The airborne would attempt a rescue.

We were chuting in thirty-eight miles behind enemy lines. A tank-infantry column of hard-driving ground forces was expected to break through to us, effect a link-up within five days. The briefing officer stood before an overlay map. Fingers traced grid lines, pointed out reported defensive positions. We got an image of the program, understood it vaguely through the unfamiliar technical terms of the trade.

"The drop zone will be dry rice paddies . . . twenty-one men to a stick . . . first echelon goes out four minutes after we cross the coast . . . heavy drop twenty minutes later . . . H-hour tentative for 7:00 A.M. tomorrow . . . The support drops on D-plus one . . . understand that every fighter plane in Korea is covering us over the zone . . . 'copters will come in for our wounded . . . we jump from C-82's

which, take my word for it, is good . . . better than going out the side
hatch of a DC-4 . . . any questions . . ."

Time passed quickly. Briefings, equipment issue, parachute fitting
chow. It rained heavily all day.

At 3:00 A.M. a light breakfast, slimy eggs, crackers, hot coffee. Rain
still thundered into the mudholes as the regiment moved out. It was
very dark. Blind dark. Riding a six-by we passed long columns, slipping
slogging through ankle-deep mire on the road to Kempo. Our headlights
picked out silent figures, company after company, weapons reversed
dungarees black with water, wet helmets casting reflections. Faces
ghost white in the darkness . . . moving up. Riflemen . . . machine
gun squads . . . mortar men . . . bazooka teams . . . recoilless
heavies . . . aidmen . . . heavy packs . . . airborne line troops . .
We wondered how they could jump with such weight.

At the field hazy cow-like shapes, each with a double tail jutting stiffly behind, rose out of the mist. Hundreds of them. Numbers, red and large on their sides. Finally B-31, B-32, our ships. We climbed down, stood shivering in a ragged line under the wings as unseen voices called off names, the order in which we were to jump.

Delay. Postponement. Feeling relieved . . . guilty . . . angry. Rain weights and slows the silk of the chutes, allows them to present too good a target.

Dawn, wet and gray, showed small bent figures clustered at the field's edge. Men moving their bowels, repeatedly urinating, trying in their nervousness even when nothing would come.

Take-off time, set for 11:00 A.M., again comes and goes. The field is still soaked in. Troops had lain in the mud under the wings for eight hours. A jeep splashed down the line. Sky clearing. H-Hour is to be at 2:00 P.M. sharp.

Half an hour and then we form in the twin lines of our sticks. Chutes, two apiece, are passed from the plane. A back or main chute, small reserve one across the chest. A mass of straps . . . girding . . . looping thigh . . . shoulders . . . groin.

Riggers wearing green baseball caps moving about tugging, tightening, talking.

"Don't worry, boy . . . it'll open . . . if it don't, come home and we'll give you your money back."

Weighted, constricted, bile in mouths, we push, are lifted, struggle aboard the plane, sit in two rows facing each other. In the center, a long row of chuted green-canvas containers. Bundles of light supplies going out with us.

Doors slam, we are imprisoned, motors cough, propellers biting into air. Vibration . . . floor bouncing . . . we are airborne.

Look at your watch . . . one hour and fifteen minutes to the D-Z. Stare at the faces around you . . . doze. Forty-five minutes . . . hot . . . sweating . . . freezing . . . sick . . . man across from you vomits . . . yellow spittle hangs across the webbing of his chest . . . doze again . . . try hard, think . . . half a comic page *Stars and Stripes* comes down hand to hand . . . staring hard, unseeing as Li'l Abner scampers through Dogpatch . . . twenty minutes . . . sick again . . . watching them out of the corner of your eyes . . . they peering owlishly back . . . far end two men yelling to each other over the motors . . . voices . . . "Yeah at Arnhem, went in with the Red Devils . . . better than the Normandy deal . . . no trees" . . . ears shut as the plane

127

goes down . . . "must be crossing the coast" . . . ten minutes . .
crew chief brushes past, hand mike trailing . . . opens door in the
fuselage on each side . . . dismal sky, wind . . . faces you . .
mouth opens . . . a bus conductor lecturing the tourists . . . "go
four minutes to the buzzer, boys . . . lotsa' luck . . . see you all or
the ground, I hope" . . . stand up . . . hook static line to overhead
wire . . . plane banks . . . slows as if brakes had been hit . . . level
off . . . loud buzzer, red light winking . . . wondering . . . "it i.
true . . . the Colonel really goes out first from the lead ship" . .
bundles in the center moving forward, swaying, leaping . . . hand or
static line pulling, sliding . . . body sideways, scraping up the aisle
legs in the lockstep of a chain-gang . . . man before you turning
diving . . . glimpse of sky . . . ground . . . tiny figures in white

running, zigzagging far below . . . "hell of a lot closer than the 750 feet they said" . . . mind trying to remember a million things, trade secrets, make it easier . . . trying . . . think . . . holding nothing . . . a blank . . . stomach heaving . . . The journey is over.

A split second of falling, body curving up . . . legs out at a 45 degree angle . . . winds . . . terrific jerk on the shoulders . . . head snapped back, eyes open . . . follow the shroud line up to the big silk canopy above.

Feet swing body on a giant pendulum . . . wild kaleidoscopic

views . . . sky filled with planes . . . brown tilted world coming up
swiftly . . . crazy angles . . . red, blue, green, jungle camouflage
chutes drifting all around . . . sudden silence is deafening . . . noise-
popping sounds drifting up . . . recognizable, burp guns . . . gooks
there . . . one more swing . . . glance at the brown mass rushing up
. . . rice stalks . . . smashing jar . . . ankles, knees buckling, head
slamming ground . . . "God" . . . you are down.

You look about Firing rattles sharply . . . people . . . things
plunge out of nowhere, slam into the field on all sides . . . make heavy
crumphing noises . . . valley . . . hills all around.

You twist . . . turn . . . unclasp, struggle . . . lay back. At your
right . . . two men . . . one standing, walkie-talkie across his shoul-

der . . . calm voice . . . "Firefly to able one . . . I have a 75 recoilless ready for firing," a tinny answer comes back, assured, definite. "Able one to firefly . . . You are released to targets of opportunity." Other man, bending low . . . pulling shells from a pack . . . moving . . . trotting, creek bank there . . . others with the big rifle . . . in the hills, people ripping cloth, familiar . . . something says, "our mortars" . . . wonder "Jesus, how can they get at it so fast . . . just getting out of our harness and there they are" . . . pros . . . last straps off . . . rising, head spins, aching . . . rope burns across cheeks, chin, back of the neck. Things slowing, familiar, settled, anticlimactic . . . routine now.

We saw wave after wave of paratroopers running, advancing through the high grass, fanning out in three directions towards the hills. Smoke bloomed up and the steady crackle of small arms fire reached out to us. Chutes, ruptured containers, debris lay everywhere. In the distance, almost obscured by smoke, was Sukchon.

We looked up. Overhead, everywhere, jets . . . criss-crossing in a pattern of cover, their machine guns and rockets lancing out, pounding the hills around us.

In the distance bees droned . . . grew louder . . . louder. Cries, "get out . . . get out . . . Christ . . . comes the heavy drop." Sky filled with giant chutes two and three to a package. Unbelievable, unthinkable things . . . crates . . . jeeps on platforms . . . a cannon, ponderous . . . more of them, a whole battery of 105's, coming in air mail special delivery. We huddled against the creek bank as they crashed around us. Rats . . . trapped, scurrying in the D-Z. Some chutes didn't even open up at all. Others, streamers, didn't hold up their heavy loads. They slammed into the earth, burst . . . threw pieces high into the air. Surprisingly, most seemed to make it all right. Men ran to unbind them. Jeeps began moving out. Gun crews dragged the fieldpieces away.

On the right, purple smoke sifted up. A signal for the CP group. We started that way. Halfway across passed a line of gooks, hands clasped on top of their heads, white peasant cloth flapping loosely about them. Prisoners. Two paratroopers, bayonets prodding, hurried them onward. One turned, grinning Irish face.

". . . dropped in on their whole damn regiment . . . never seen anything like us, I bet . . . changed clothes . . . find their uniforms lying all over up there," he said. We found the CP. Colonel Frank S. Bowen and his staff on a hill, holding papers . . . plotting . . . point-

132

ing out across the valley . . . making their plans. Flag going up. Our banner now the furthest north.

Dusk . . . bunching up . . . prisoners from the compound digging us a hole . . . wide, deep . . . a voice cheerful, sarcastic.

"Christ . . . that ain't a foxhole . . . it's a mass grave," from a figure standing shadowy on the rim of our home.

We slept. Peaceful. Our airborne artillery pacing the hours with intermittent fire. All directions. Good. Keep the gooks down.

Two days. Another drop in the morning of each. Helicopters come in. Took out our wounded, big baskets hanging on their sides. Street fight in a village up the road. Interesting . . . CP moved to a church. Rumor that the gooks were coming in that night. They did. Gunfire . . . feet shuffling in the darkness outside . . . voice, scared, fighting panic . . .

". . . what's left . . . K company . . . overrun us out at the railroad tracks . . . sixty-three left, I think." More gunfire . . . louder . . . closer . . . gooks in the drop zone. We got ready to move suddenly, gripped weapons. Figure outside rose up before us . . . big

BAR spoke long, proudly. Figure sank back down. Gunfire died away. Dawn found streets dotted with dead people in white peasant clothes. These paratroopers were sharpshooters. One company did get it bad though. Had been overrun without warning; they suffered heavy casualties.

Radio message came up from Sunchon. Battalion had got to the prisoners. What was left of them. Had found eighty-nine of our people. Atrocity again . . . bodies stacked, hands tied, piled in a railroad tunnel. Apparently they got the rest away the morning we waited to jump.

Noon the third day. Burial of our dead. One in particular, big, blond, young . . . rigid . . . eyes so blue and staring. We wrapped them in parachutes, dropped the bundles of the Airborne into a hole in the ground. Voice of the "jumping padre" raised in the requiem.

Four P.M. afternoon of the . . . rd. Much noise to the southwest. Firing. Sound of motors. The tanks have broken through.

bAyoNETS

bEfORE sARiwON

It was night and very cold. We had been on the road for sixteen hours, jeeping our way forward from Seoul. We had crossed over the parallel at dusk. Now even in the darkness dust rose around us as we drove behind and around long convoys of armor. The shapes of the men who rode them loomed large against the flaming skyline.

The column moved slowly. Ahead and on the sides could be heard occasional gunfire. It never seems to get any closer. The big tanks and gun carriers stretch down the road behind us, looking solid, permanent. Briefly, as if seen in a flash of lightning, they leaped from their obscurity when passing a burning hut. Then momentarily, as with all things military, there was no uniformity. Guns, turrets, the faces of men who rode them, all became clear, sharp and alive as individuals. Then just as quickly they were gone from the light and the night was seemingly the darker for their passing.

Gunfire talked back and forth in front of us. Bumpers smashed together and tank motors stalled as an angry voice whipped out at the column, "Cut that, you dumb sonsabitches."

Then moments later, the same voice, "I said 'cut that,' we're the support."

The silence was abrupt, as if all sound had been cut off as simply

136

as by a twist of a control button. In that silence up ahead an unknown voice spoke, blurred, vague, querulous, and couched in a nasal twang. He heaped obscenities on our leader. He spoke of this in detail as one who addresses great throngs and is aware of his audience. Then descending to the basic four-letter words he rendered his summation, decreeing his contempt for all tankers, the army, the world, the universe. It seemed we had not forewarned this sentinel of the gloom of our approach. We moved forward. The dim outline of a hole appeared, was seen on a little ridge beside the road. A 3.5 bazooka lay on the edge. On the far side a figure sat. Calm and dignified, the unknown voice had turned his back to our world.

This was the outpost of our bivouac. It was the command center for a regimental armored unit elected to lead the assault on Pyongyang. We rolled into the usual schoolyard where all Korean command posts are located. Vehicles cluttered the area. It was a familiar home. Inside,

137

the floor was just as uneven, just as littered as the floors of a hundred
other Korean schoolhouses we had seen turned into a hundred other
command centers up and down the length of this land.

Outside the dusty road for the first time in many hours was empty.
It gleamed dully in the moonlight. Pyongyang lay just fifty-seven miles
over the hills. A tank coughed briefly down the valley, its echo bounced
back with a harsh throat-clearing of gun metal. Things stood still in the
room, breathing, air, the glow of a cigarette. Time is the eternity that
begins with a sound which makes your guts, in a fraction of a second,
force bile into the mouth in a coppery-tasting spasm of fear. When no
answering voice of authority spoke back from over the hills, we crawled
into a corner and slept.

Dawn still comes early in the fall. The air was crisp as we turned
out together. All around us men were rising, first picking up their
weapons, then shoes, maybe a canteen, and going out into the schoolyard.

Garbage pails filled with hot coffee steamed outside. The cooks had been up before us. The chow, coffee and crackers with a strip of bacon tasted good. The air was loud with the familiar curses, obscene yells, clicking of rifle bolts and other noises with which line troops habitually greet the new day in their reverence. This was a top outfit. No one had washed too recently, most had beards and looked rough, worn and very professional.

Tankers are tough people, a unique breed. Hairy and hard, ears constantly deadened from the roar of heavy motors and quite often shaken about as fleas on a dog. Generous with their ammo, they are loud and profane. They prefer the company of their own kind.

Motors began to idle and the big radio aerials swayed against the sunrise as the word came down to prepare for the day's work. Tankers sat atop the turrets, feet dangling inside, bits of breakfast still matting their beards, staring up the north road, thinking their thoughts.

We went back into the schoolhouse. Someone had tacked a large torn map on one wall. The colonel, unshaven and slightly stooped, stood before it much in the manner of a father about to lecture his children. His fur parka was carelessly thrown over his shoulders as a cape. The staff stood about. They and their colonel seemed on intimate and familiar terms. He addressed nearly all by nicknames or just "you." He kept saying while tapping a finger against the torn map, "We take this deal over, do just like Al would."

No one bothered to explain who or what "Al" had been.

The colonel mumbled on about details, obscure things, but seeming of vast importance to his men who frequently asked him to repeat, "Just when do we drop off the riflemen, sir?"

"How we gonna take any prisoners with no extra space, Colonel?"

And mostly "Do the air guys know which tanks are ours today?"

The colonel answered all in detail. Then he announced that ours was to be a special assault up the north road to seize a place called Sariwon. He called it "our mission to Sariwon." He told how the capture of this vital North Korean industrial area which was responsible for manufacturing most of their army equipment would open the door to the enemy capital of Pyongyang only thirty-five miles further. Prisoners had admitted that the big stand for the capital city would be made on the heights before Sariwon with what force could be mustered from their retreating army and that if we pushed them from that place there would be no defensive fight for their capital. We doubted this very much at the time but it later proved correct.

Moving out in a column of tanks, infantry clustered about their sides like olive-drab grapes in a vineyard of steel, we soon came to our first objective. A place called Mulgaeri, filled with burning mud huts and enemy snipers. First warning came in the outer approaches when a British trooper tumbled from the turret of the lead tank, a bullet in his brain. We heard no rifle report over the sound of tank treads. Riflemen jumped off, began to fan out and advance. Almost immediately the sniper was flushed and taken alive, scarcely a few feet from the road. A hungry sullen-looking little man dressed in the ragged remnants of an enemy uniform, he glowered at us as we ran up.

By now the troopers had deployed on either side of the ridge line bordering our road. Tanks were bunched up and firing down the defile, throwing white phosphorus into the town. Buildings flared and smoke billowed up. We saw no figures but they were in there. We drew mortar fire. No casualties. Things happened fast. Orders came, the troops went off the ridge and fanned into the town in columns on either side of the main street. Tanks paced them in the center, the 50cal atop the turrets spraying the side streets while the infantry fired into the buildings and ahead. Smoke at first was pretty thick. Figures constantly moved. To stand still was to invite a bullet.

We went through with the first platoon. In the center a cement bridge crossed the usual small river. Slugs whined off the heavy pillars as the lead unit ran across and spurted down the street anxious to reach the suburb and the flatlands once more. Taking a town for the assault unit is always a matter of fighting a way up the main drag to get out of the city in the soonest possible time and taking the minimum number of casualties. Support units backing you up always fire the city and clean out the sidestreets. Time passed. A succession of running, crouching in dusty doorways, watching buildings burn, moments of laughter as a Tommy slipped in a sewer opening, moments of fear as a man again tumbled wounded from the tank beside us. Seemingly in a short time yet somehow a long time, we were on the outskirts and once more in the flatlands. Behind us the town was now really afire and rocking with gunfire as support tanks and infantry tore the place to pieces. We were glad to be leaving.

The column moved forward. More towns were passed, all without encountering resistance. Our air had been working far ahead of us, blasting with bomb and rocket the town targets for the day. For 121 miles above the border along the main road are smoking heaps of rubble where once had been enemy cities. The smell of burned thatch

143

145

and the stench of charred dead are a familiar odor to troops moving north. Fields are littered with white warning notices to the people that air attacks are coming, to evacuate their homes. All look the same. They all smell the same. And after assault by our air they all die the same. Skies always seem gray on entering them. The few remaining walls cant crazily against a smouldering skyline of drifting ashes. Occasionally a citizen is glimpsed hurrying about on some mission amid the ruins. Maybe to salvage his possessions, or his home, or maybe his family. All things appear riddled and gashed as if from the slashing blows of a giant knife fighter. You move rapidly through these places. The machine gun atop the lead tank is enough fire power for the moment to appease the walking infantry and to keep off any vengeance-minded gooks.

In one such place, a factory area, a giant wooden "peace arch" reared into the sky spanning the road. The traditional crossed Russian and North Korean flags gleamed dully out from the peeling paint. The building beside it was decorated with large pictures of Stalin and the president of the enemy republic. The tanks and troop-laden trucks roared under the arch and past us. Soon everyone was shooting, at the picture on the wall behind us, just for the hell of it or out of good spirits. Bren guns roared, then some of the wilder American drivers ferrying the British troopers began to steer past with one hand and cut loose with their revolvers with the other. High yells and catcalls echoed over the sound of the motors.

Dust puffs walked up and down the walls around the picture. Neither fell. Odd but no one appeared to fire except at the picture of Stalin. Apparently in the minds of us all he was "the enemy" and as an Australian with us said, "The other creeper is just some gook biggety."

Soon a rifleman ran inside, upstairs, leaned out the window and pulled loose the picture of Stalin. He came from the building and as the next tank roared up out of the dust clouds his hand reared back, the

picture sailed out into the roadway. Giant treads mashed it into the dirt. Troopers waved and yelled. He grinned at the boys hanging alongside the big steel sides as it rocked up the highway and they smiled back. No one thought to look down at the mangled picture in the roadway. It was a happy time. Happy times were scarce on the point however. Our people must never think of this push as a grand sweeping affair of giant convoys of armor heading north. Always let them remember that up ahead, far ahead, in the lonely stretches and amid the little flaming towns, men with long rifles and fixed bayonets are walking behind the lead tanks, fighting and dying on the road to Pyongyang. They make up what is known as the "point." A human shock absorber. A lonely life, a deadly life. Behind may lie the massed firepower of an armored column, but ahead lies Indian country. Country belonging only to the enemy and the dead. Country which can only be bought with the blood of foot soldiers.

Place names mean little, foreign sounding, odd to the ear, but Mulgaeri, Sinmak, Kuamni and Younghyeni will forever remain vivid to the troopers of the U.S. 1st Cavalry Division and the British-Australian brigades with whom we went up that north road.

The column had rolled forward all day, the heavy tanks forming a steel screen to pass the infantry through the towns. Usually they were greeted by rifle and machine gun fire from enemy snipers left behind. They took their toll. Here and there at little obscure places, villages of thatched huts or sometimes merely a turn in the road, a tankman would roll from his turret, shot through the head, or a riding rifleman would slump over the treads, blasted down by flanking fire from the ridgetops bordering the road.

Our last objective, Younghyeni, was cleared with minimum difficulty. We encountered only token resistance. Halfway through we picked up two commies, both garbed in peasant white but with enemy uniforms in briefcases slung over their backs. Cycling along, seemingly oblivious of the arrival of our armor, they drew suspicion because of the newness of their bikes. Anything new, be it physical or mechanical, is suspicious and unusual in Korea. We left them, hands upraised, stripped and shivering beside the road in the custody of a single rifleman. We rolled past, stared hard at their cotton pants, drooping dejectedly below naked shanks. Wondered what the townspeople who stood behind the two thought of this scene. Their leadership for communism had led only to this—standing naked in the dust, shivering and prisoners, as the armor of an enemy rolled forward into their land.

149

Our Australian driver coughed, rasped, "Hope they freeze their bloody arses off," as leaning far out from the moving jeep he pursed lips, expelled a spumy gobbet of spit to the feet of the unclothed ones.

At the far outskirts time slowed for a moment. Tired, dirty riflemen jumped from the tanks for a stretch. Water gurgled in upraised canteens. A few ate cold rations. Then General Allen, ADC of the 1st Cavalry and task force commander, jolly, round-faced and smiling, passes forward. He and the chicken colonel who rode the turret of the lead tank confer briefly over a map. They remind one of two elderly, benign professors planning some scholastic course. They make pointing gestures, reshuffle the map, nod their heads. Neither smiles for a moment, then they yell something, unheard over the roar of tank motors, the general slaps at the colonel's shoulders, runs back, vaults into his jeep with the big 50cal. In a moment the colonel is back in his turret. He, like a football coach, gives a circle wave with upraised arm and then points down the road. The column moves forward. We came to the hills outside of the place known as Sariwon in the late afternoon, and it was here that we met the enemy on ground of his own choosing. They were in strength. First warning came when rifles cracked from the hillside orchard flanking us and about two hundred yards off the road. We couldn't see the town but knew it was just over the ridge to our front. We drew fire. Everyone took cover. They stopped us cold. General Allen, pushing his jeep behind the lead tanks all day, was as usual in his forward position. He jumped out, stamped up and down on the road in a little dance of anger, waved his map, kept yelling in a high demanding voice.

"Godammit they're in that orchard, rake 'em, dammit, blast them to hell out of there."

His face got red. He waved up his aide from the jeep. The aide clambered up the big treads, trained his field glasses on the orchard to give fire direction to the tankers. Other tanks around us buttoned up and moved forward. The infantry lay in the ditches. That approaching armor must have confused the gooks for they gave away a perfectly hidden defense position. Suddenly we saw figures tiny in the distance running across the slope centering the orchard.

They must be trying to get back farther to the ridgetop. The general is now coolly pin-pointing them with his own glasses. We draw more rifle fire, most of us are in the ditch, but he leans negli-

152

gently against a tank steadying his arms on the tread. In seconds we are blasting the orchard with all guns. The fire we have been getting slackens and stops. We, on the point around the lead tanks, can now kneel with comparative safety and watch what, to a foot soldier, can be no more pleasant a sight: his own heavy weapons pinning down a visible enemy. The big 90mm rifles of the tanks fired pointblank into the orchard while the 50cal on turrets searched under the apple trees walking their slugs up and down the slopes. Soon riflemen were out from the ditches and on the flanks. A spotter plane is overhead dipping his wings to indicate the presence of troops in strength on the upper ridge. Suddenly, with a rush, a great mass of gooks cross the open center and vanish on the upper ridge line. Two more, apparently wounded, straggle across.

We cannot dislodge them. We begin to draw more fire. An hour has passed. Air support can be called but might take time, and the general wants us passing through the town by nightfall. A direct frontal assault by infantry on the orchard is decided upon. Enemy fire momentarily slackens. A squad strength patrol goes out, we follow them with the telephoto as they walk up toward the lead tank about seventy-five feet from our ditch. A volley comes from the orchard and the patrol is down. Two men are hit. The tank officer has been wounded in the face as has one of the foot patrol. The assault company starts out. We go with the lead platoon. Midway to the tank we hit the ditch, sliding, rolling, falling into its safety as fire comes from the apple trees across the road. Men crouch on one knee, move forward in a wary sliding motion. The lead tank crawls off a bit down the road

to let us have flank fire support, a few assigned riflemen creep beside it. The word is passed down the line that in seven minutes we assault the orchard.

We look at the faces of the men around us. These are troopers of the British Brigade, tough, sun-blackened and full of fight, fresh from the jungles of Malaya and Hongkong. This is a company from the renowned Argyll and Sutherland Highlanders, a regiment which has fought England's wars for centuries past. They speak in a strange jargon completely understandable only to themselves. A fiercely proud and wild lot, they disdain to wear helmets in battle, many not even bothering with garrison caps. Heavily armed and well trained, they exhibit a dash and vigor for their work equalled perhaps only by our Marines. We feel that among them we are a match for any troops in the world. They are truly professional killers, the cream of service shock troops.

They show little emotion. Some are quiet and calm but most talk, smile and throw small jokes to each other in their weird tongue. Their bayonets are wide and long, they stroke them, fondle and caress the barrels of their many automatic weapons. Many are garlanded with grenades. A hairy corporal a few feet from us sits at his ease in the ditch bottom, makes light of the "two bloomin' camera fellers!" and others down the row take up the rib with smiles. It is easy to see that they are pleased that we shall go in with them. We feel proud and very flattered. Our seven minutes seem to drag out. Then suddenly, orders. The corporal is twisting his head to the man on either side, rattling something out in a fast blurred monotone. Now men are on one knee, tensed, etched against the dust of the roadway. With a fine high yell they are up out of the ditch and running forward across the road, jumping the other ditch and moving over the little field to the orchard. A steady roar of fire cracks down the line. The heavy boom of support

from tanks on the road echoes amid the rattle and burr of machine guns from the convoy down the valley. We find ourselves running forward in the company line. We are at the edge of the orchard. Tank fire has slackened, and the men fire through the hedge and move in at intervals. They weave up through the trees covered with freshly ripened fruit. We look up momentarily. Strange that the gay little apples bob so freely in the wind. Around us figures indistinct and fast-moving, dart about at angles. We are down, dragging ourselves, one knee on the ground and the other leg pushing us forward. Around us the Enfields of the British crack sporadically. There is mute evidence to the accuracy of our support fire. Enemy dead litter the area, many of them practically ripped apart by the high explosive shells from the tanks. Two gurgle and kick slightly. A Tommy puts his rifle close and the heavy cloth jackets smoke as the lead passes through. Better to leave no enemy wounded to your rear in this war.

Ten feet from us a running Tommy stoops, jerks a rifle from beneath its dead owner, hefts it above his head, the sling bespattered with the brains of its former possessor. He vanishes with a yell. Soon we are at the far end of the orchard where a hedge bars our advance across the field to the ridgetop. Brambles tear at our clothes. Eagerness and momentum of the initial assault dies. We drop flat and crawl, feeling heavy and weighted. Hands, feet, the bulge of a helmet, seem twice larger in size. A single enemy machine gun from the ridgetop to our front rakes down the hedge a good three feet high. Leaves from the apple trees about us drift down, his only victims. The men lie closely, poke their rifles across a dirt pile. Down at the end of our line a radio man, portable set strapped to his back, mutters soft nothings into his mike. A moment later tank fire rockets overhead and we hug the ground. We hear the machine gun no more. A light mortar crew plants their little tube at the edge of the field in front of us, and as the tiny shells whistle up to thud on the ridgetop, we move out in groups of three and four, at intervals of twenty feet, slipping through the tall grass to the edge of the field.

From the valley below it seemed so small. Now it stretches out an immense and impossible distance. A long, long way. We crawl out past the line of troopers. Their young blond officer rises slowly. He bends slightly and yells a string of epithets to his men, he tells them that they shall rise once more and cross to that place and that they shall seize it and hold it. He is very impressive. In a moment all are on their feet again, leaning forward as men will do in a strong wind.

Their bayonets lance out at a thirsty angle, they make savage chopping motions with them, they near us. We raise the camera, now they are running. We see a snarling expression, lips back over teeth. Again comes their fine high yell as they sweep past, every man firing as fast as he can pull trigger. The final objective, the hedge fence atop the ridge, looms up and we flop down against its protection. Suddenly it is wonderful to feel the soft wet earth. The contour of the plowed field seems to just fit the curve of our bodies. Everyone is thirsty. Canteens come out and talk struts up and down the line. We strengthen our position. Men begin to dig in behind the hedge. The young officer, oddly enough, looking just as Hollywood would expect of the typical British subaltern, crawls past. His blond mustache flutters as he mumbles, "Thought I had blasted kidney trouble when your blasted American ka'bene came apart in my hands during the last crossing."

His horn-rim glasses flicker as he crawls down the line dragging the broken weapon in one hand. He motions to his radio man, talks to units on the road below. Moments later announces that the company is to hold the ridge line until the convoy passes through and then fall back to join the rear element, thus preventing the gooks from hitting our support vehicles. As we are an independent armored column actually operating about fifteen miles in front of the main force, we can easily be cut into from the rear if not protected. The officer says another company is coming up to support us. Enemy fire is sporadic and very high. Apparently when they saw our bayonets they moved out fast and far. They now lay down only harassing fire. Our casualties were light. Amazingly light from what we had expected when the orchard loomed up. One man killed and five wounded, but one of those being serious. Only one fell near us, receiving a rifle bullet in the chest. All were taken in the orchard. Moving so quickly we had hardly noticed our flank where they got it. We had them behind for aidmen.

Two hours have passed. We hear the tanks start on the road below. Their motors growl harshly, mingling in the guttural chorus of a long-familiar rhythm. Time to rejoin the column.

The dead soldier rests on a stretcher just outside the line of apple trees. Someone has covered his body, placed his Enfield with him and packsack alongside. Momentarily, as always, we wonder who and what he had been. At the roadside they carry a badly wounded man out to the aid jeep.

A Tommy comes walking down from the trees with a child in his arms. One of its hands is almost severed by shell fragments. He has

wrapped a rag around the baby's body and presses the arm tightly as he walks. A moment later two soldiers bring in the mother on a stretcher, face down and badly wounded. Shrapnel nicks dot her body with bloody gashes. She and her child had chosen to go with the enemy of the orchard. Perhaps one of them had been her husband. These two living were found among the ripped dead in that place. As we move out we pass the young soldier, the child screams in his arms. His eyes swing to the tank for assistance. He looks confused, even pained. Plainly this is something Army regulations or jungle training in Hongkong has not prescribed for. We don't know what to say to him, so look away. Our driver mumbles something to himself.

Up ahead lies Sariwon. Its outskirts smoke vaguely in the twilight as the first tank rumbles down the road. The jeep seat feels good as the tires crunch over the stones on the trail to the north. We wonder how long we will have to go.

POSTSCRIPT

bivouac

ONCE, far above Pyongyang, in the hills shrouding another shattered village, we lay in a ditch with our rifle people while they speculated idly, as all men who lay in ditches waiting and clutching their weapons will do, of things, and times, and places. Rumor had it, a new kind of fighting man was fronting us. A strange one, with yellow skin, higher cheekbones, more slanted eyes. One who wore padded cotton clothes. Some said he was Chinese, down on a people's crusade. It could only be idle rumor. Our foot soldiers, these men who carried their own arms, had thrust forward bayonets to the far north, and all Korea was nearly ours.

Above us the air sighed, and the earth grunted to itself in metallic groans of pain as corps artillery put up a preparation. Armor rumbled in the distance. Fifty yards or so to the front, hardly visible, lying flat, a line company waited on orders for a jump-off. Artillery faded. In the silence, remote, unmistakably separated from anything else, a single gunshot sounded back from the valley, plodded weary and dejected up the ditch and across the waiting rifles. All the misery, the fear, the terrible loneliness of those people and their place can be echoed in the sound of slow fire on the line. Close by, somewhere real close by, were sleeping things that had been gook infantry. The air was

164

foul, reeked with the acrid nose-stinging odor of rottenness that announced the dignity of enemy dead. Those in the ditch paid it no heed. Obviously. It, like the slashed earth, the noise, the constant ache and tiredness of body, like the faces of their own wounded, was a pattern of life. Any other would be strange, alien.

Down the road, wintry sunshine slanting across the dust whirls, came a KMAG jeep. Three impassive Korean faces stared as it ground to a stop. The driver dismounted, walked towards us. He was an American officer, probably one of the few left from that small band of Army people who had been assigned to South Korean units prior to the invasion from the North. Most of them were either dead or prisoners since those first bitter June days when Korean fought Korean across the parallel. The silver bars of a first lieutenant gleamed softly from worn combat jacket. Big, dusty, gray-headed, long overdue for both a shave and sleep, he approached the trench, stopped, stared down, inclining head quaintly, almost bowing in polite query. Words coming in a soft drawl, asking which way was "foward." The rifle people seemed almost unsure. Pointed confusedly to a crossroad in the distance. He got back in his jeep, a long leg draping over the side, inquired politely again, "Which way did you say was the right one?"

A somber-faced infantryman slouched in a hole, spoke across chested rifle, "Don't rightly know, lieutenant . . . but all them roads end the same," concluded, "where you goin'?"

The KMAG officer sniffed the air, puffed cheeks, grinned widely, his words carrying clearly, "going no'th . . . going no'th to dip ouah swords in the waters of the Yalu." Only an old expression. An expression that those gray men possibly in his past had used so long ago in their war. The Koreans made no movement or sound, only looked straight ahead as he gunned the jeep, rattled off.

In the gully, scratching sound of bodies shifting on gritted soil . . . clicking of bolts . . . long silence . . . talk.

"Jesus, what a craphole this is!" from a figure wallowing in the ditch bottom. Above him, another, rags, long rifle, tired eyes. Murmuring, "You just aint ashittin', brother." Continuing irreverently, "You know . . . you know, that Albert was the best fukkin' BAR man we ever had, and all that yellin' he done, an' the way he could work that tool." Wondering querulously, to the ditch bottom, "Do they put crosses on 'em down there?" Getting no answer.

Ahead and at the flank, booming of light mortars, authoritative insistence of small arms. Unseen voices yelling things to each other. On the slope people stooped up out of the earth, peered sullen and disapproving at the ridgetop. Hunched over, moved out in a thin line. The assault company went forward. Those in the ravine stirred, rolled on stomachs, rested heads in arms. Watched. From the ditch, voice again, "No Alberts with them people," persisting, "Yeah . . . a damn good man." Shifting, rolling the perforated barrel of a light machine gun against the bank, wiping at its oily smugness, spitting on the road, his eyes sliding across the paddies and over the hills that are Korea. Finishing slowly, weary whispering of thoughts.

"Yeah . . . they was all good men."

Spitting again. Looking off down the empty road. Turning. Muttering words to himself. Face blank. Looking to the slope. Seeing that other place over the ridge line.